You're the
PRIZE,
Not the
CONTESTANT

You're the PRIZE, Not the CONTESTANT

A Practical Guide to Dating & Finding Love for Women of All Ages

Pam Johansson

NEXT CENTURY

PUBLISHING

You're the Prize, Not the Contestant

A Practical Guide to Dating & Finding Love for Women of All Ages

Copyright ©2017 by Pam Johansson
All rights reserved.

Published by Next Century Publishing
Las Vegas, Nevada
www.NextCenturyPublishing.com

ISBN: 978-1-68102-257-4

Printed in Canada

CONTENTS

Introduction

After listening patiently to one of my angry rants about men and dating, a good friend of mine responded with, "You're the prize, not the contestant." I didn't fully comprehend what he was saying at first; I assumed it had a negative connotation since my friend was, after all, a MAN. Whoopsie! But after hearing him out, I realized it was meant as a compliment. I'm the prize? That can't be right. Perhaps the reason I've considered myself to be a contestant in the dating arena for most of my life is because the ratio of women to men has been three to one in every place I've ever lived. If you do the math, that means you're competing against two women for every one man, right? UGH!

Case in point: When I was in college, I met and began dating a man during the first semester of my first year. I was young and naïve and thought we were exclusive right out of the gate, since that's how it worked in high school. I was completely smitten with him and was certain the feelings were mutual. Imagine my surprise when I saw my new boyfriend kissing another woman one night shortly after we began what I thought was an "exclusive" relationship. I was devastated and wasted no time in confronting him. I'll never forget the excuse he gave me that night. He looked at me ever so seriously with his innocent blue eyes and gorgeously chiseled face and said, "The ratio of girls to guys at this college is three to one, so why would I ever tie myself down to just one woman?" Apparently, it came down to basic statistics. I had no rebuttal for this very logical explanation, so I explained to him that, while I appreciated his grasp of statistics, I don't like to share. Next!

Now that I'm older and wiser, I have learned that you're not really competing with anyone but yourself. Yes, there will always be someone prettier, smarter, thinner, and funnier than you, and there may be more women than men in your area, but there will never be another YOU. You are an original. You are amazing. And the man who wins your beautiful heart will be eternally grateful for picking door number one, for YOU, my darling, ARE the prize—and don't you forget it!

Now, let's get back to business. Have you ever heard the expression "those who cannot do, teach"? Well, that's the very premise by which I operate. Right or wrong, it's the truth; I feel very knowledgeable in the area of dating, but I admittedly suck at execution most of the time. I don't want to scare you off right out of the gate, so let me assure you that I KNOW how to execute and will gladly share my secrets.

I once told a co-worker that I was being blown off by someone I really liked, but I could reel him back in by the end of the day with my magic formula if I so desired. She knows me to be a fairly modest person most of the time and looked at me in disbelief. I showed her the "blow off" email from him that I had just received and she agreed with my take on things: he was gently, but obviously, rejecting me and saying, "Have a nice life." I asked her if she believed I could lure him back in and get another date with him, and she said, "No." Suffice it to say, she's someone who doesn't exactly sugarcoat the truth to spare your feelings.

I crafted a brilliant response full of confidence, indifference, flirtation, and intrigue, showed it to my co-worker, and hit "send." Within an hour, he responded playfully and excitedly and asked to see me again on Saturday night. Easy peasy. My co-worker was dumbfounded. She asked me how I knew I could turn things around, and I told her it was based on "a LOT of experience." I was able to execute that time just to make a point to someone, but I am oftentimes weak in the presence of a highly desirable prospect.

Just because I suck at execution doesn't mean *you* have to suck at execution. I'm here to instill in you the confidence and tools you need when it comes to dealing with the opposite sex and finding lasting love. I recognize that many have tried to do this before me and may not have succeeded, but I am hopeful that my experiences, passion for helping others (YOU), and ability to communicate will give you the tools and the motivation you need to be successful in love.

Okay, so what's the problem? Our SELF-ESTEEM, or rather, the lack thereof! I have talked with countless women over the years, all agonizing over whether or not he would call, and whether they should make other plans or wait until he called (just in case he wanted to do something). The questions are all too familiar: Does he like me? Does he love me? Why hasn't he called? What did his text mean? What did *he* mean? What should my next move be? Is he going to propose? When will he propose? It goes on and on and on. I have had many male friends over the years and have NEVER, EVER, EVER heard them stress over these things. That's not to say they don't, but if they do, they're certainly not as obvious as we are about it. They just do their thing, seemingly without a care in the world, and we just sit back and TAKE it.

Don't get me wrong, I'm not saying men don't have insecurities about women and relationships, but let's be honest: we are the weaker sex in this area. Always have been. Always will be? NO! I'm here to change that! Maybe it's because we were taught to be submissive at some point, or maybe our religion or role models taught us that the man is the head of the household and should have ultimate decision-making power. Whatever the reason, it is causing us much undue stress and leaving us powerless on the relationship front. We need to take that power back so we can cultivate relationships that are based on trust, mutual respect, honesty, and compromise. Oh, and YOU can't be the only one compromising, young lady!

So, what qualifies me to write this book? I would say first that I have had an inordinate amount of dating experience due to the fact that I have been single most of my life, open to meeting new people, and actively engaged in the process for many years. All that to say, keep *your* dating "experience" to yourself: don't brag to your new man or prospect about your extensive history with men. Contrary to what some women believe, it will NOT make you seem more interesting or appealing. The man with whom you're speaking will be busy tallying up your bed partners in his head as you drone on and on about your prolific dating past, and he'll be wondering how the hell he will ever measure up. In keeping with the all-too-familiar and annoying double standard, he may also be thinking you're a whore. He instinctively knows that you share all of the details of your sexual encounters, good or bad, with friends, acquaintances, and even family, and that you will compare him to all the rest. Even if you tell him you've only slept with three people in your life, he will assume you have bedded every single man you've ever dated and whose name you've uttered. There is no winning with this game, so it's best not to get into too much detail about your past. Just . . . DON'T.

I have learned many lessons the hard way (my M.O.) and want to make sure others learn from my mistakes. I have also struggled with insecurities for most of my life, which have carried over into my dating life. What else? I have a Master's in psychology and had a two-year stint in the field of counseling, which has armed me with more insight into personalities and relationships than ever before. I did all sorts of counseling for all sorts of reasons, and I won't bore you with the details, but I excelled at couple's counseling and found it fascinating and extremely rewarding to unravel the issues and work with individuals to heal and strengthen their relationships. So are you ready to get on this train with me? I promise it will be worth the ride!

Me, Myself, and I

Step one in this process is making sure you're comfortable in your own skin and are content with being single. Are you the kind of person who enjoys your "freedom" when you're single? Can you survive Valentine's Day without a man and without drowning your sorrows in a pint of cookie dough ice cream while watching Bravo for twenty-four consecutive hours? And more importantly, do you LIKE yourself? I mean, do you REALLY, honestly, genuinely *like* yourself?

If the answer to any of those questions is "no," you're susceptible to what I like to call "Filler Dating." That's right. FILLER Dating. Are you guilty now? Have you been guilty in the past? Have you kept some poor unsuspecting puppy around for too long just to avoid the deafening silence in your life? Yes? Well then, how, young lady, do you expect to meet "the one" if you're already in a relationship? A true gentleman with good morals and values is not going to actively pursue some other guy's gal. It also goes against guy code. So be brave, say "so long" to the filler guy, and be okay with being alone.

Conversely, have you been someone else's filler? You may not have wanted to admit that to yourself, but you probably knew you were just a filler, willing to stick around waiting and begging for crumbs. It doesn't feel good, does it? But in a filler dater's mind, it's still better than NOTHING. So, if you don't like being someone's filler, then don't make someone *your* filler. In doing so, you're selfishly holding each other back from meeting "the one."

I know what you're thinking: he may not be Prince Charming, but he's better than NOTHING. Let's talk about that word. If you're single, does that really mean you have *nothing*? Well, that's up to you. If you want to sit home wallowing in your singlehood instead of building a life for yourself, then you might truly have nothing. But, if you take advantage of those times by going out with your friends and doing things for yourself, then it's not *nothing*. It's quite *something* and quite valuable to get to know yourself and learn to enjoy time to yourself. And the beauty of learning to enjoy time by yourself is that you will, by default, set the bar a little higher in the man department: because you're having so much fun with me, myself, and I, you will not be as willing to risk rocking the boat by having another guest join the party.

The other pitfall you're susceptible to if you're not enjoying the company of me, myself and I is overlap dating. This is when you're so afraid of being alone that you won't let one guy go until you have another on the hook and fully secured. What's wrong with this scenario? Besides the fact that you're letting your co-dependency show, you're also cheating on someone in this scenario.

Years ago when Internet dating starting becoming popular, I joined several sites, intent on fully putting myself out there in every way with the hope of finding true love. My naivety led me to believe that all others on these sites would be like me: SINGLE, AVAILABLE, HONEST, and serious about finding love. Not the case! While many most certainly fit the criteria, there were plenty who did not.

I remember one of my friends telling me she was going to sign up for e-Harmony shortly thereafter. I should have been excited for her, but I was, instead, baffled. She was in a long-term relationship with someone whom she cared for but had doubts about. She thought it would be helpful for her to sample some other goods before making her decision to end her relationship. My contention with this? She did not advertise herself as someone who was already in a relationship, nor did she tell her current boyfriend that she would be dating other people. I couldn't help but think there were men out there doing the same thing and that I would inadvertently find myself in the middle of a convoluted love triangle in my quest for love instead of meeting up with another clear-minded, SINGLE man. Not okay! My golden rule is always to do unto others as you would have them do unto you. If you live by this, you will make good decisions MOST of the time.

I learned a long time ago that if you're contemplating dating other people while still in a relationship, you're in the WRONG relationship and need to end it first. It's that simple. Something is missing, and you're too afraid to take that leap from your safe, comfortable, mediocre relationship into singledom, which brings me back to our "me, myself, and I" discussion. It's so much easier to take that leap if you've learned to enjoy time with yourself. You're awesome, you're great company, you get to make all of

So get to know YOU. Get to LIKE you. And stop thinking of "single" as a bad word.

the decisions, and the possibilities are endless when you're not stuck in a dead-end relationship. Another bonus? You don't have to shave your legs every day when you're single. This has been one of my favorite perks! Just sayin' . . .

So get to know YOU. Get to LIKE you. And stop thinking of "single" as a bad word. You must truly love yourself first in order to be ready for and recognize Mr. Right and to know, without a doubt, that you deserve the best and should never settle for less!

Love Thyself

In keeping with the "me, myself, and I" theme, it's imperative that you love yourself before you go on a quest to find someone else to love. There is no magic potion you can take in order to love yourself, but there are many steps you can take towards developing a healthy self-esteem. Rarely have I met a woman, myself included, who is truly comfortable in her own skin. We tend to be very critical of ourselves (and each other) despite our many assets. This might be due to our upbringing or the fact that we're always comparing ourselves physically to one of the Kardashians. Perhaps someone in your past or even present has caused your self-esteem to plummet due to emotional or physical abuse. (Dump him!) Well, it's time to reprogram your brain to start being nicer to you and to learn to love yourself unconditionally.

It's imperative that you love yourself before you go on a quest to find someone else to love.

Years ago, I bought the book *Self Esteem for Dummies* and was absolutely mortified when my handsome Belgian boyfriend found it. I couldn't even look him in the eyes when he found it. In fact, I felt my self-esteem drop even lower at that moment. Having a man find your self-help book collection is like walking into Target in nothing but your underwear on the Saturday before Christmas. It's your worst nightmare. Fortunately, he was one of the good ones and not only minimized my embarrassment, but wrote a blurb in the back of the book that helped me more than anything in the book ever could:

"This guide is a complete waste of money. You are the most beautiful, funny, intelligent girl I have ever met!"

Ironically, years later when I met the man who would later become my ex-husband, I was in a book store with him and his son when he picked up that very book (not knowing I already owned it) and said mockingly, "Hey, Pam, you need to get this!" He then laughed at his own cruelty, knowing he had hit a nerve. That was just one of many ugly jabs I took from him over time and will never take from any man ever again. This brings to mind an amazing quote by Eleanor Roosevelt that you may have heard: "No one can make you feel inferior without your consent." When you believe in yourself, nobody can make you feel badly about yourself. You simply will not give your consent to—nor will you tolerate—someone treating you that way.

Men who ridicule or belittle you are simply trying to bring you down so they can feel superior to you. It comes down to their own insecurities and need for control. Whatever the reason, it is NOT okay, and you need to steer clear of men that put you down in any way. It's very difficult to climb back out of that hole once you're in it, and he will do everything he can to keep you there. I know from experience.

Let's get back to how we foster this seemingly elusive confidence. It's about loving yourself inside and out, figuring out what's broken and why, and doing everything possible to fix what's broken and better yourself. Everyone is a work in progress, and we should never stop looking at ourselves honestly and regularly so we can continue to make positive changes. So where do you start?

Start with your past. What has happened to you in the past that hurt your self-esteem? Do you have unresolved conflicts with family members? Did you have a bad experience or traumatic event that shaped who you became? Do you have a fear of intimacy? The best place to start delving into all of this is in the presence of a trained counselor. No, a counselor can't FIX you, but a counselor can help you identify those dysfunctional elements of your past that drive self-defeating behavior and show you how to come to terms with your past and move forward. Church is another place you can go for support, to learn to love yourself and know that you are loved. Many non-denominational churches are very non-judgmental and have speakers that know how to reach people on a deeper level and inspire them to be their best.

Loving yourself physically is important too. What is it you don't like, and what options do you have for changing it? Do you need to tighten and tone? Do you need to lose weight? Do you need to clear up your skin? Go to a gym, see a doctor, see a dermatologist, get a great hairdresser, etc.! Specialists are out there for everything these days, and there's no reason why you can't take advantage of them (except budget, but if that's not an issue, go forth and hire a specialist). I'm not saying to go schedule a facelift or get shots of Botox every week. In fact, please try to age gracefully so you can still express yourself! It's a slippery slope, so start with the inside and the rest will follow.

Are you self-aware? If so, write down the qualities about yourself that you don't like or wish to change and make a conscious effort to change them. Baby steps! If you're not self-aware or are not sure if you are or not, ask a few of your HONEST friends to tell you what you need to work on. That's a scary thought, but it will help you in the long run. If you have been the recipient of some criticism by a man, ask yourself if there is truth to it. If you have heard the same criticism from more than one man, chances are it's something you need to work on.

It's also important to surround yourself with people that love and support you. Unfortunately, if you're a giver by nature, the takers will find you. They will take take take and suck you dry. They will use and abuse you without remorse. Although you really enjoy giving to others, this pattern will eventually take its toll on you if you don't find balance. Healthy relationships involve give AND take between two people that alternate between giving and taking. Even a giver needs to take once in a while. It can be exhausting always being there for others and not having anyone to lean on in return. Every now and then, you need a rest, and you need someone to take care of YOU.

Take a good look around you, and ask yourself if the people in your life are good *to* and *for* you. If they're not, you need to distance yourself from them and find people who build you up instead of tear you down. If you have a good support system, you will feel less alone and may be more inclined to hold out for a good man instead of begging for table scraps.

Love yourself—deeply, truly, genuinely—and you will start to attract the right kind of man. If you continue to secretly loathe yourself instead, you will attract men who are controlling, abusive, and selfish. And what's worse, if you have children witnessing this, they will think it's okay. Your daughter will think it's okay to be controlled or abused. She will think it's okay to take care of a man who isn't taking care of her. She will think it's okay to be someone's doormat. Your son will think it's okay to treat women disrespectfully. He will think it's okay to control and abuse them. He will think it's okay to do what he wants whenever he wants in a relationship instead of putting the other person first. It's not okay. It's NEVER okay. Love thyself.

Attracting the Right One

Do you ever wonder why you keep ending up with the same type of guy? Why, even when you feel like you've detected your self-defeating patterns and are looking for a different guy, the SAME guy keeps finding you?

Well, here it is. You are putting out a certain vibe that attracts a certain type of guy. A controlling man isn't going to be attracted to a secure, confident woman. A secure, outgoing man isn't going to be attracted to an insecure mess. An insecure man isn't going to go for the prettiest most confident girl in the room. An abusive man is going to look for a weak, submissive woman. I think you get the point.

So, it's important to know what you REALLY want, and then think about what that kind of man wants in a woman. I learned over time that I attracted confident men when I was out with friends and feeling my most confident, but I attracted controlling men when I met them in other environments where I was feeling shy and uncomfortable.

It's important to know what you REALLY want, and then think about what that kind of man wants in a woman.

I know I will get some flak for this, but even the way you dress makes a statement about you and will attract a certain type of guy. I had a friend years ago that used to dress very promiscuously and would always attract sleazy guys looking for nothing but a one-night stand. They would see the low-cut top, miniskirt, fishnet stockings, and heels and think, "We've got a live one here." Conversely, if you go to a social event in khakis and a loose-fitting turtleneck, you might attract the geeky scholar in the bunch. That's fine if that's what you're looking for, but it's probably not going to work if you're looking for someone who is edgy and fun. Again, don't try to be someone you're not just to get a man, but be aware of the non-verbal messages you're sending to the opposite sex by way of your clothes, makeup, body language, actions, companions, etc.

Have you ever had one of those wonderful gay male friends? That elusive male who seems to really "get" women and is loyal to you to a fault? He compliments you just as your friends might, but it feels better somehow because it's coming from a man. He's easy to talk to and makes you feel a little less single when you go out. You might both be attracted to the same man, but you'll never have to compete for the same man. He can give you valuable insight into the male brain and is an incredible judge of character.

Well, I had such a co-pilot for many years and enjoyed my time with him immensely. He filled a void that my girlfriends just couldn't fill. I loved him for so many reasons and still do. The only problem was that he was mistaken as straight by most. What's wrong with that? Nothing if you're not out with him and trying to find a man. You see, my friend, no decent man is going to approach a woman if he thinks she is on a date with another man. Even if your gay friend is the best wingman ever, nudging you into the best-looking guys in the place, and giving you the confidence you need to approach someone, he is unintentionally, unknowingly, and unequivocally P-BLOCKING you. If you don't know what that means, ask one of your friends.

And more importantly, if you're attracting men while with another man, one they THINK is straight, you may not be attracting the right kind of man. He might just be someone who likes a challenge or someone who likes the idea of sneaking around when one or both of you is already in a relationship. He just might be interested in you for all the wrong reasons.

No, do not ditch your amazing gay friend. NO, NO, NO! Just make sure there are other people with you when you go out so that you don't appear to be a couple. Or, you can do what we did and start talking to each other loudly about Mom and Dad so the people around you think you're brother and sister. Genius! The only problem with this little stunt is if you meet someone that overheard the two of you, and you end up having to fess up about your fake brother later on.

No matter what your type, just be aware of *his* type and understand what message you're sending to the people around you on a daily basis. If you're a "loser magnet" or a "geek magnet," ask yourself "why?" Once you figure out the *why* behind it, you can learn to send the right non-verbal cues out into the universe and soon become a "GREAT guy magnet." Imagine how awesome that would be? Your biggest problem would be determining which great guy to date. Utopia.

The List

Okay, admit it. You have a list. You do, don't you? Whether it's simply a mental list or a written list, it's still a LIST. I have witnessed the Millionaire Matchmaker tearing up people's lists, and I understand where she's going with it—especially with long lists—but I still think it's important to have one.

What do you want? What do you need? What is it you CAN'T live with? What is it you can't live without? While the old adage "opposites attract" has some truth to it, the likelihood of two people with nothing in common having a long and happy relationship is small. What if you're an outgoing person, and he's an introverted computer geek? Worse yet, he likes to sit in his underwear for hours, watching loud, obnoxious, gory action flicks, and you're dying to go to a friend's cook-out, but he won't leave the couch. You like together time, and he likes to have a guy's night out . . . every night of the week. You love animals and grew up with pets, but he's allergic or doesn't care for them. Will you be happy without the unconditional love of a dog or cat for the rest of your life? And let us not forget the most important of all subjects—children. Does he want children? Does he already have children? Do you? If one or both of you have children, are you each willing to take on the role of a stepparent?

Far too often, we let our hearts and libido do all the talking and ignore our heads. If the chemistry is there, the logic typically goes right out the proverbial window. DAMN, he's HOT! What? He's an unemployed ex-convict with eight kids and five ex-wives? Keep your head in the game, ladies! Trust me when I tell you—that voice in your head is your friend and wants what's best for you. That voice, although sometimes whispering ever so faintly and oftentimes in an annoyingly self-righteous tone, will tell you when to run, and it's almost always right. Unfortunately, you treat that voice like a schizophrenic third cousin and forge ahead, refusing to heed the warnings, for all the wrong reasons, don't you? WTF?!

I remember my mother once comparing me to another young woman my age during a brief dry spell in my dating life; she seemed to have no trouble finding men, while I, on the other hand, did. True dat. HOWEVER, that other young woman was game for anyone, at any time, and didn't seem to have a type. Her type was a living, breathing man. That may be fine for recreational dating if you're not the picky sort, but it's not fine for everyone. I informed my mother that the other woman had significantly lower standards, which inevitably led to a larger pool of men. My pool was much smaller thanks to that all- important list. I like to think of myself as a strategic dater as opposed to the all-too-common recreational dater, but to each his or her own!

My point is this: if your list is too long and too specific, and you're strictly adhering to it, you may very well miss out on something or someone wonderful. BUT (and there's always a "but") if you have no list at all, you may find yourself spending time with people who are not suitable for you at all for the long term. For example, if you're dating someone who has expressed to you that he never wants to get married and doesn't want children, but that's something you want, you may be wasting your time. If you're dating for fun, who cares? If you're dating to find a husband, *then it matters.*

> **If your list is too long and too specific, and you're strictly adhering to it, you may very well miss out on something or someone wonderful.**

Sadly, marriage is no longer the sacred institution it once was, but that doesn't mean we should enter into it light-heartedly with the intent to bolt at the first sign of trouble. That's not fair to you. That's not fair to him. And it most certainly isn't fair to any children the two of you have brought into the mix either from previous relationships/marriages or together. While children can be resilient in many ways, they can also be emotionally fragile, and no child wants to be shuffled back and forth between two parents.

One piece of advice: take physical attributes off the list. While physical attraction is important (otherwise, you would just have a buddy), it can come *after* you've gotten to know someone a little better. I have met people that I've had absolutely no physical attraction to and fallen hard for them after getting to know them, even seeing them as handsome months later. Conversely, some of those beefcake, eye-candy types can quickly lose their appeal once you get to know them. Yes, I have a physical type, but I have fallen in love with men who didn't even come close to my perfect physical description. I'm not saying someone you find repulsive will suddenly look like Ryan Gosling to you after he opens his mouth, but there are a lot of average Joe's out there who become incredibly appealing once you get to know them.

The rest of the list comes from really knowing yourself and knowing with what you can and cannot live. Think about things like religion, morals, values, child-rearing beliefs, etc. Let your heart drive, but keep your head in the passenger's seat in a car that has a brake pedal on BOTH sides. You feel me, dog? And no, you should not take that last comment personally. I'm simply a cool chick with a very geeky, inappropriate, and sometimes questionable sense of humor.

Emasculation Proclamation

In this day and age, most of us unintentionally and unknowingly emasculate men, further limiting our chances for a lasting partnership. I don't care what they say. They are intimidated by our success. Yes, most men truly want a confident woman, and yes, many men will welcome—with open arms and an open wallet—the perks that come with two incomes. However, they still have an inherent need to be needed. If we just want them and don't *need* them, that's simply not enough for most men.

So what's my point? Do I think you should dumb it down so you can land and keep a man? Hell no! Go conquer the world, sister! But, when you're done doing that, make sure your man knows how much you appreciate his ability to contribute to the relationship in other ways. I'm going to be a little stereotypical here, so forgive me, but many of us are NOT handy. (If, like me, you fall into that category, raise your hand. Is there someone next to you right now giving you funny looks? It might be the title of the book and not you raising your hand that's piquing their interest, but who cares.) Ask your man to help you lift something heavy or fix something in your home. Recognize his strengths, and let him help you where you need help. Did you hear me? LET HIM HELP YOU! For some reason, we are so hell-bent on being independent that we are afraid to ask for help. It might expose a weakness. Well, guess what? We all have weaknesses and limitations, and that's okay. We will stand on a wobbly kitchen chair trying to hang a picture by ourselves instead of asking for help. We will hire a handy man to fix something instead of asking someone we know for help. We'll say "I've got it" instead of letting him help. We need to stop!

I'm one of those fiercely independent women who has scared a man or two off with my successful career and was angry and resentful when it happened. Angry at men. Angry at myself. Angry at the intellectually challenged, helpless, beautiful women who lured my man in with their boobs instead of a brain. It just made me angry—that is, until I started to view it differently and understand it.

Several years back, I went on vacation with a friend of mine just a year out of college and headed to Myrtle Beach, South Carolina, with her. Both of us were ready for trouble. I was still in college mode, wanting to go out every night, so that's just what we did. Unfortunately for us, every bar was also in spring break mode and hosting bikini contests. It was a necessary evil that we endured only because that's where all the men were. If you've ever been on spring break in a vacation destination, you'll understand!

As someone who's always interested in what makes people tick, I couldn't help but notice that the women in the bikini contests were always introduced as teachers, librarians, or nurses. I don't recall hearing any of them say they were doctors, lawyers, or CEOs. Then, in a crazy twist, a girl we saw win a contest the night before in another bar got up on stage to join a new contest, but this time, she was a nurse, not a kindergarten teacher. Ah-hah! BUSTED! But she won again anyway.

I'm not sure what she did for a living in "real life," but I thought even more about it all after that. Men are not usually threatened by teachers because they work with children and are seen as very nurturing—a good quality for prospective wives and mothers. Men also see nurses as very caring and nurturing; how perfect they would be in the home. I haven't figured out the draw to librarians (and I'm not sure they even exist anymore), but I realized that the professions being used in the bikini contest were chosen because of their appeal to men. Now, I'm no fool. I know that the hot body with the perky boobs was the FIRST thing all the *men* noticed, but *I* couldn't help but notice that the professions the women MADE UP were ones that would not be intimidating to men.

My next observation was the reaction of men when I progressed from the modest title of "trainer" at work to the more formidable title of "Associate Director of Merger Integration." I was SO proud of myself and wanted to shout it from the rooftops, but I quickly realized that men ran from this title. They hated it. They feared it. They ran from me in a way that had never happened before. They expressed interest and made advances towards me, but they changed their tune as soon as I told them what I did for a living. If you've ever watched *Sex and the City* (best show in history, in my opinion), you may remember the episode where Miranda went to an Eight at Eight type of event to meet men, but they lost interest every time she said she was a lawyer. However, when she decided to say "flight attendant," she was met with a completely different reaction (albeit from a guy who also lied about his profession, but that's beside the point). That scenario is exactly what I'm talking about. It's disappointing and doesn't say much for the evolution of men, but it is our reality.

A few years after my post-college spring break trip, I became friends with a local attorney. She was fun, bubbly, and incredibly intelligent. She was married to a wonderful man and appeared to have it all. I started spending more and more time with her and her husband and noticed that she was a bit of a nitpicker. She was, shall we say, OCD clean, and he was . . . well, kind of a slob. They were opposites in many ways. One of the things I began to notice was how hard he tried to please her and how hard she was to please. Do you know anyone like that? Is it YOU? Is it someone you know? Think about it for a moment, and be honest with yourself.

I remember walking through their front door with her one day and seeing him standing there with a big proud grin on his face. He had cleaned the entire house without being asked to do so. I likened it to a ten-year-old boy trying to surprise his mom with a good deed in the middle of the school week. I was ready to applaud and give him the positive reinforcement he so obviously needed and wanted when my friend proceeded to pull the toaster oven away from the wall on the kitchen counter to point out the crumbs, questioning why he didn't think to clean under it instead of just around it. He was totally deflated and visibly hurt. I was in total shock.

Why, why, why did she have to do that? Why not focus on the positive and thank him for what he did, thereby rewarding and even encouraging good behavior? Psychology 101! Why would he continue to try if he was just going to continue to be met with criticism? I normally keep my mouth shut when in the midst of a domestic dispute, but I had to say something. I waited until he left the room and told her that his version of clean would NEVER equal her version of clean and that she needed to cut him some slack. That didn't go over very well.

A couple of years later, I received a call from my friend, and she was hysterical. Her perfect, adoring husband had cheated on her. She was in shock and was even more upset about the person with whom he cheated than the act itself: "A SECRETARY!" she yelled. Then she went on to question why he would cheat with a secretary when he was married to an attorney. Huh? It all made sense to me, but in her mind, he had taken a few steps down the proverbial ladder, and she couldn't figure out why.

Well, you're here for a reason, so let me share with you my theory. *He found someone that looked up to him*—and he liked it. He found someone that made him feel smart, worthy, and needed, and he went for it. He was married to someone that made him feel small, unworthy, unneeded, and totally inadequate. I'm not making excuses for cheating, and I feel very strongly about that being the deal breaker of all deal breakers, but I am pointing out the obvious: If you don't treat someone well, they will eventually find someone else who will.

> **If you don't treat someone well, they will eventually find someone else who will.**

She wore her profession like a badge of honor, yet it had no power in the relationship arena. None. In fact, her superior attitude hurt her, and it hurt her relationship. Just remember that when you've been at work, running the show all day long, and you come home to someone. You're no longer at work, and you should be on equal footing at home.

Do NOT lie about your profession (or your age or anything else for that matter). Just don't make it the forefront of your conversation with a man. Once he realizes you have many other layers (nurturing, caring, fun, etc.), you can let him know that you do okay at work. If he can't handle it at that point, he is not your guy! We should never make ourselves appear smaller to allow someone else to feel bigger. Rather, we should simply highlight other assets in order to attract a man instead of focusing on our successful careers.

Preparing for the "Job Interview"

If you can't go to a job interview and convince the hiring manager that you are valuable, capable, and desirable, you probably won't get the job. The same is true in the dating arena. You have to truly believe in your worth and sell it! And that's only after you've decided you want what *he* has to offer too.

Men will say over and over that they want a confident woman. Many of us will answer that want ad and lie our asses off to get the job. We may get it, only to lose it shortly thereafter when they realize we falsified our resumes. This is a waste of time for everyone involved.

So once we have the "job interview" or that first date secured, what do we do? First of all, you need to find out where he's taking you and dress accordingly. This one is a no-brainer. Do *not* wear your 6-inch CFM pumps to the bowling alley. Do *not* wear your favorite yoga pants to a five-star restaurant. (I don't care how great your ass looks in them; don't do it!) The key here is to dress the part and look fabulous without overdoing it.

You have to truly believe in your worth and sell it!

I once asked my roommate to give me a make-over before a date. I was really excited about the date and wanted to knock it out of the park in hopes of securing another date. She agreed, without soliciting a lot of detail about the look I was going for, and happily began painting my face. When she finished with the war paint, I saw my barely recognizable self in the mirror. I looked good, or so I thought at the time, but I didn't look at all how my date remembered me when we first met. Actually, I looked more like a drag queen than the girl next door that I had professed to be. The unprecedentedly bold, electric-blue eye shadow was quite a stark contrast to my normally muted and slightly contoured brown eye makeup, but I went with it.

Unfortunately, my new look wasn't exactly a hit. My date actually commented on my makeup at some point during the date, and not in a good way, which was absolutely MORTIFYING. I was so caught off-guard that I outed myself. Yes, I confessed to having my roommate give me a make-over (bad move). As soon as the words left my mouth, I regretted them, thinking "now he knows I tried too hard." I was embarrassed and wanted to run and hide, but instead, I threw my friend under the bus, telling him she did a terrible job and I simply didn't have enough time to fix it before our date, nor did I want to hurt her feelings. He told me it was nice, but just not me. Epic fail!

You definitely want to "wow" him in the looks department since men are such visual creatures, but you don't want to go out and get false eyelashes and a boob job before your first date. Be you. Be your *best* you, and make sure you've allotted plenty of prep time on the big day so that you can bring your A game.

So what if the big day arrives, and you're sick or getting sick. Should you still go on the date? Absolutely NOT! Take it from me, the person that made that mistake *once*. I had a date lined up with a guy I had met while out and was extremely excited about it. I bought the perfect outfit and planned to dazzle my way into a second date, and ultimately, his heart. Unfortunately, I caught a cold just before the date. I felt awful, but I was determined to go anyway. I gave myself plenty of prep time and a hefty dose of cold medicine while I waited for my date. I had convinced myself that, with enough cold medicine and nose spray, I would feel fine and have a sexy raspy voice instead of the nasally voice I had the day before. I stashed some tissues in each pocket, some nose spray in my purse for back-up, and was on my way.

My date took me to a nice Asian restaurant where I proceeded to sniffle and cough uncontrollably throughout the meal. Not only did I irritate the other patrons, I thoroughly disgusted my date. NOBODY wants to be across the table from a sniffling, sneezing, hacking germinator, and

NOTHING screams desperate like a woman who, instead of postponing the date, goes out sick as a dog instead. Hindsight is wonderful, but foresight is your friend!

So what else should you do in preparation for the big day? Well, if this is someone you've met on the Internet, I would suggest going back through his bio to brush up on the details and find some conversation starters. It's easy to inadvertently dominate a conversation when you know nothing about the other person or when you let your nerves take over. In your mind, you're just giving him information so he gets to know you, and you're also avoiding awkward silences. That's fine, but how will *you* get to know *him* if you're doing all the talking?

Think about that one friend you have that you just can't live without. What is that special quality he or she possesses? I have found that people are drawn to people that make them feel good about *themselves* or bring out their best side. If you're doing all the talking, it doesn't make him feel good about himself, nor does it bring out his best side. While you're droning on and on about your challenging job or difficult roommate, he's probably thinking about how to end the date politely so he can move on to the next. It should be give-and-take, just like a conversation with anyone else. Ask questions to get to know him, and listen intently. Hopefully, he will do the same, and you will establish a healthy dialogue that will leave both of you feeling good about it and wanting more.

Do not, under ANY circumstances, spend the evening talking about what a fucktard your last boyfriend was. Yes, I said *fucktard*. Would you badmouth your last company or boss while in a job interview? I certainly hope not! The interviewer needs to see that you're a positive, glass-half-full kind of gal. So does your date.

If your first meeting happens to be at a restaurant that your date selected, do NOT make any negative comments about the venue, the waiter, the waitress, the food, etc. Doing so will only make him feel bad about his selection or lead him to the conclusion that you're high maintenance and impossible to please!

When the check comes, don't get into an arm wrestling contest with your date over who is going to pay it. If he asked you out, then *he* should pay for dinner, and *you* should be gracious and appreciative, thanking him when he does. If there's an awkward silence when the check is put down, you may want to address it and offer to pay half. I have only had *one* man out of *many* take me up on my offer to pay half. This man asked me out, picked the restaurant, and then proceeded to complain incessantly about the prices on the menu throughout the meal. When the check was delivered, he excused himself to go to the restroom. Oh yes, he did. NOT COOL! He was obviously hoping I would take the hint and pick up the entire tab. Not a chance. When he returned to the table and ignored it, even after the waitress picked it up twice and returned after realizing there was no money in it, I finally put him out of his cheap-ass misery and offered to pay half. He lit up like a Christmas tree and gladly accepted my offer. That was our first and last date.

And now, for the end of the "interview." This can be extremely awkward, even if the date went well. You may both be struggling with what to say and wondering if there will be a second date. Whatever you do, do NOT go home with him or take him home with you! No funny business on the first date, young lady! Leave him wanting more in every sense of the word. Some people don't even think you should kiss on the first date, but I think that's just silly. If the chemistry is there, and you're both down for it, by all means lock those lips and see what kind of kisser he is. That first kiss can be very telling and can also be wonderful. Enjoy it!

A great closing statement can go a long way in an interview and on a date. If you really like the guy, close it with confidence and with the assumption that you WILL see him again. Do NOT say, "I know you probably won't call me again, but I hope you do because I really like you a lot," unless you are trying to expose all of your weaknesses and exude a lack of confidence. Instead, try, "Thanks for a great night. I look forward to meeting up with you again." If the date ends a little more intimately with the two of you lip-locked for an hour outside of your car, you don't need to be so formal. Tell him you had a great time and need to go home to take a cold shower. Always leave with him wanting more!

If you're just not into this guy, and he asks you out again at the end of the date, you need to decide if he's the kind of guy who can handle rejection. If he is, tell him you enjoyed the date and are flattered, but you just don't think the two of you are a match. Regardless of how gentle you are in your delivery, his ego will be bruised, and it will be a tough moment for you both. (Potentially hurting someone's feelings is never easy.) If you think this guy is a loose cannon and may go off on you if you reject him, then tell him you have to check your schedule and will let him know about getting together again. He may not get the message, but he can at least convince himself that you're really THAT busy and accept your excuse for the time being. After that, it can go one way or another: either he gets the hint after one or two unreturned calls, or he doesn't and requires what I like to call the sledgehammer blow-off.

I went on a date once years ago with someone I met a few weeks earlier through friends. I knew without a doubt at the end of the night that I never wanted to see him again. He was nice, but he came on a bit too strong for me, even telling me on the way home that he was driving slowly so that he could spend as much time with me as possible. I knew he would want to see me again based on his comments and actions throughout the night, so I spent that very slow drive home formulating my escape plan. I was leaving home to start my senior year of college a couple of weeks later, but I told him I was leaving the very next day. I'm an honest person in general, but I felt that a lie was my only way out of this. He asked for the address there so he could write to me, and I told him I didn't know it yet. Somehow over the next week or two, he managed to talk my mother into giving him my address, so when I arrived at my off-campus home, there were *several* post cards from him thanking me for a great date. I knew then that I had a problem.

After months of unreturned phone calls, my stalker still didn't get the hint and persisted. In keeping with my fear of confrontation and desire to avoid it, I continued to screen my calls until Thanksgiving, at which time I returned home to see my grandfather who had just suffered a massive stroke and was in the hospital. I was devastated about my grandfather's condition and had forgotten all about my stalker when my parents' phone rang one afternoon. I was about to leave the house with my sister to go to the hospital but stopped to pick it up. It was him. The Stalker. The guy that I went out with ONCE back in August. The guy that, after 30 or more attempts to contact me, simply did not get that I was not interested. The first thing he said when he realized it was me was "Boy, you sure are hard to get a hold of." Are you %$#&%* kidding me? I lost it. I delivered the most epic, totally warranted, unrelenting, harsh, and long overdue sledgehammer blow-off ever bestowed upon anyone. I still remember screaming into the phone and wrapping up my rant by telling him that I would contact the police if he ever tried to contact me again.

Guess what? It worked. I never heard from him again. Should I have handled the issue three months earlier when it began? Absolutely! Would he have accepted a white lie told in an attempt to spare his feelings? Probably not. So, if a sledgehammer blow-off is warranted, let 'er rip, and don't wait three months to do it.

The bottom line is that you should always be ready for your "interview," and put your best foot forward. You might learn that you don't want the job after all (and should be upfront and honest at the time of the offer). Or you might not get selected for the role. Regardless of the outcome, you need to prepare in advance and execute flawlessly.

Waiting on the Call/Text

You've been out with Mr. Wonderful, and it was epic. There was no shortage of chemistry or conversation, and you just know he could be "the one." You can't stop thinking about him and have told all your friends about him. You have gone into nauseatingly endless details about your date(s) to anyone who will listen. You're in it to win it. Now what?

Ladies, this is the moment where we have given up our power and need to take it back! No matter what year it is or how much gender roles change and evolve, men will probably ALWAYS prefer to pursue a woman and want a bit of a challenge. It's in their DNA. So when you drop your plans, your friends, your kids, your cats, your dogs, your whatever, to go out with them when they call, they lose interest. Why? Because you're too easy, too available, and too needy!

This scenario is so hard to navigate because when you're really excited about someone, you can't wait to see him again. There are only two days in the weekend and other people in our lives. How many times have you cancelled on a friend or family member to go out with a guy? I'll bet you have done it. I have done it. My friends have done it. Their friends have done it. When is it okay to cancel plans to go out with a guy? NEVER! Do you think your guy is going to cancel his weekly poker game or his night out with the guys for YOU? Not likely. Once you commit to a plan with someone, the right thing to do is stick with it. Don't drop someone for the bigger, better deal under any circumstances. It's just not nice and very inconsiderate. If it has happened to you, and odds are that it has, you know how it feels. Now you're stuck home alone because your friend had something or someone better come along. Ouch.

Do you really want to go watch another chick flick with your BFF Saturday night, or would you rather let your new man wine and dine you at the best new restaurant in town? I know the answer, but if you've already committed to your BFF, you need to politely decline your man and tell him you would love to do it another night. (Otherwise, you risk him thinking you're not interested.)

So what do you do in the meantime? You stay busy, and you make plans like you always did. If Mr. Wonderful is as enamored with you as you are with him, he will make an effort. I'm *not* saying fill your calendar up a month in advance, because most guys aren't going to wait that long to see you, but I *am* saying don't hold the weekend open for him if it's a Thursday and he hasn't called or texted you yet.

The other side of this equation is that part of you is looking for reassurance, which may lead you to text or email him just to gauge his level of interest. Don't do it. Sometimes we're trying so hard to win a man over that we forget our own worth, not recognizing that he should be trying to win *us* over too. It goes both ways, so stop being so available! The man who wrote the book *He's Just Not That Into You* is a genius. It really is that simple sometimes. I had a man tell me once that he really liked me, but he wouldn't date an "OTP" woman (which means *outside the perimeter* in Atlanta and translates to the burbs). I laughed and said, "I had a man from Belgium fly here to date me, but you're not willing to drive up GA-400 for me?" He was just not that into me, and I knew it. Know your place, and don't fight for someone who isn't fighting for you.

Don't fight for someone who isn't fighting for you.

Indifference Makes the Heart Grow Fonder

Have people ever told you you'll find him when you're not looking? What the hell are they talking about? How are you going to find something you're not looking for? And why can't you look for him? This goes back to men loving the chase. It's in their blood, and it makes us crazy. This is not all men, of course, but it does represent a large majority of them based on my findings.

If you're desperate to find a man and are on the hunt, they will KNOW. They can smell it! Your friends will know. Strangers will know. I have seen women that are looking for men, and they primp constantly, look around at their prospects, and pretend to be interested in what their friend is saying when they're not. They use their keen peripheral vision to check out the guys to their right and left while nodding politely to their friends, pretending to be interested in the latest funny cat story.

> **If you're desperate to find a man and are on the hunt, they will KNOW.**

They dress the part, look the part, act the part, and EXUDE the part. Meanwhile, who are the guys interested in? That girl across the room having a genuinely good time with her friends—the one who hasn't even noticed them and doesn't really care if she goes home alone or not.

A friend of mine and I were in Vegas one weekend, in search of debauchery like everyone else, and found ourselves at a popular nightclub. We were a little older than the rest of the crowd, but we had reached that point in our lives where we just didn't care and were there to have fun. We were surrounded by stunningly beautiful young girls in tight-fitting skimpy clothes, but we were not there to compare or compete. We just wanted to dance and have a good time, and it wasn't long before we attracted the attention of two handsome Australian men. They were, in my opinion, the best-looking and most interesting men there, and they couldn't get enough of us. We broke away to go to the restroom at one point and stood looking in the mirror at ourselves, surrounded by a sea of beautiful girls. I laughed and wondered aloud, "How did we get the two best looking guys out there?" My friend pointed back to the mirror where we could see the reflection of the beautiful girls primping madly and anxiously while the two of us looked light, fun, and completely indifferent. She said, "Just look at us. That's why!"

We were indifferent when it came to finding someone that night, and men everywhere sensed it and loved it. What is this all about? It isn't just the chase men like, but also the lack of pressure from an indifferent girl. An indifferent girl isn't talking about marriage on the first date and doesn't make the guy feel like he has to commit right away. The indifferent girl's "I don't give a shit" attitude is refreshing to men and freeing to them. They have to work to impress her and can keep having fun with their friends without getting any pressure from her to hang out. Why? Because she can take him or leave him and will not fall in love on the first date. She is slow to warm and may eventually develop feelings, but she doesn't scream "Desperate!"

I took a long hiatus from dating one year, but a visiting friend convinced me it was time to get back out there. She was the kind of friend who knew how to instigate trouble and the kind of friend you want to have when you're single. After one night out with her, I had secured two dates for the following week. I was never one to date more than one person at a time, but I decided if it's okay for guys to do that, then it's okay for me to do it.

We went out the second night with no agenda since I was officially back on the dating scene, and we met JR. JR was engaging, intelligent, and funny, but not the type of guy who would normally attract my attention. I had no romantic interest in him whatsoever, but I enjoyed his company. My indifference intrigued him, and he began to pursue me. I told him my dance card was full, but he persisted. I finally, reluctantly, agreed to go out with JR and gave him my number.

With three dates on my calendar, I was feeling confident and ready for action. My first date was with an exceptionally good-looking man who, at some point on the date, was pushing to go home with me and became frustrated when I refused. In his desperate attempt to convince me, saying "we're both adults," he also told me he went to the prom with Calista Flockhart. So . . . does that mean I should drop my pants? Um, no. NEXT!

The second date was with someone from work that we had met out the week before. I quickly learned that he was arrogant and insecure after he insulted both me and my out-of-town guests. Another fail, so now it was on to the third guy. I was least interested in JR and had only agreed to go out with him because he pressured me into it. We had some scheduling conflicts but finally set up our first date.

After one date with JR, I went from indifferent to hooked. I can't explain it, but I was drawn to his warmth and confidence. We clicked in a way I hadn't with anyone in a long time. My indifference went right out the window, and as I began to show my feelings, he inevitably began to cool off. Have you been there? This can be SOOO frustrating, but it seems to be a very common phenomenon. That being said, I think it's best to hold your cards close to the vest as long as you can. I don't fall often, but when I do, I fall hard and fast and am quite obvious. I'm also usually "falling" for a façade as are most people in the early stages of dating. It takes a long time to really know someone, so it's best to go slowly with a cautiously optimistic attitude, keeping yourself upright and alert until you really, truly know him. Then you should be able to free fall from a 100-story building without hesitation, landing in his loving arms instead of doing a face plant on the pavement like I have on so many occasions.

I remember feeling the distance between me and JR—and wondering what I could do to pull him back in—when he suddenly gave me the golden opportunity. We were sitting on my couch one night, having what I thought was a wonderful evening, when he said, "I care about you a lot but am afraid I'm going to end up hurting you." This is code for "I'm just not that interested in you," or "You're getting too close and you're freaking me out." I knew this was a pivotal moment in our relationship, and I desperately wanted to hold on to him, so I thought quickly and knew what I had to do. I looked at him confidently and said, "Honey, if you knew my track record, you would know that the chances of me hurting you are way greater than the chances of you hurting me." BAM! He laughed and looked thrilled as this previously mousy, clingy, googly-eyed girl pulled out the cocky, confident side. I could see the relief in his face and immediately felt him warming up again.

What happened after that? I couldn't sustain my cocky attitude and danced this dance with him for quite some time, even breaking up with him twice (another way to make a guy fall for you). He ended up having to take a job in another country, so our story eventually came to an amicable end.

I'm not suggesting you maintain a façade of indifference throughout the dating cycle. You have to let your guard down at some point unless you want to be known as the ice queen. But I do believe you should quell those feelings of school-girl giddiness just a tad in the beginning in an effort to challenge him and pique his interest. If you get too excited and get caught doodling your first name with his last name on a cocktail napkin in the restaurant on your first date, he will likely panic and run. If he thinks you're somewhat indifferent, he will feel less pressure, and you will look less desperate.

Giving IT away

Don't make me say IT. I might have family members reading this book. You know what I'm talking about. Oh yes, you do! It's *easy* to snag a man with our sexuality, but nearly impossible to keep a man if that's all you have to offer. It's *easy* to get attention if you offer your boobs on a silver platter, but nearly impossible to get a man to look at your face once he has that platter-o-boobs. It's *easy* to put on makeup to feel better about yourself, but much harder to love the person on the inside and sell the REAL you, not the "you" that you think every man wants.

We all know there is a double standard here. If a man sleeps around, he's just being a man. If a woman sleeps around, she's a slut. Now, if you're just someone with a healthy sexual appetite, and that's all you're looking for, HAVE AT IT, chica! (Use protection, of course.) However, if you're someone who is looking for love and are considering doing it only to please your man, then don't!

The pressure we feel in this area is real. The struggle is real! Why did I lose my virginity? Not because I was ready and in love. No. I lost it because my boyfriend told several of our friends that he was going to dump me if I didn't put out! After hearing the devastating news from one of my friends about my boyfriend's secret ultimatum, I wasted no time in telling him I was ready to do the deed. There was no time to plan it out. There was no time to light candles and play our favorite song in the background. I had to keep him, so I had to do it now. Right? So . . . I did. And I cried all night, too ashamed to even tell my friends that I had just given away my special gift. I was alone with my big secret, alone with my shame, and alone with my self-loathing. Alone. That's not how it should feel. That's not how it should go down. Pressure, from a man or from *yourself*, is never a reason to do it, virgin or not. A good man who loves you for YOU will wait. He is in it for YOU. Not IT.

I don't know if things have changed or if I am just noticing it more, but it seems like guys are more likely to ask you to go home with them than they are to ask for your number and take you on a date. A one-night stand should not be a prerequisite. Perhaps it has to do with the venue? Perhaps meeting men in bars is not the way to go? Probably not, but it's the only place where I know to go (aside from the Internet) where I can meet single men.

The last time I met an interesting man in a bar, I was reminded of why that's not necessarily the best venue if you're looking for a quality mate. I admired him from a distance, watching him laugh with his friends, and I could tell he was a fun person. He was attractive and well dressed, except for the florescent orange Crocks he was wearing. They were HIDEOUS! Somehow, I sensed he could handle my obnoxious opening line, so I delivered it unabashedly and successfully captured his attention: "Those are the ugliest shoes I have EVER seen." BAM! Please don't use that pick-up line unless you are 100 percent certain that the intended target can handle it. Admittedly, not my best work or proudest moment; nevertheless, it was effective.

We clicked instantly and spent the rest of the evening talking, flirting, and dancing. I was so excited at the thought of seeing this man again and could sense that it was mutual. So when the night started to wind down and the bartender yelled the dreaded "last call!," I looked over at my orange Crocks cutie and waited for him to ask for my number. Nope. Instead, he said something like, "So, do you want to come home with me?" Uh, no! I was so disappointed but tried to maintain my poker face. "No, I need to go home," I answered, to which he replied, "But I thought we hit it off?" "We did," I said, leaving him looking even more befuddled. Oh, boy. I knew I had to spell it out for him at this point, so I said, "Look, if all you want is a one- night stand, you picked the wrong girl. So why don't you be a gentleman and ask me for my number?" I said it with a cute little grin so as to not scare him off with bitchiness. He looked thoroughly confused and proceeded to try to talk me into going home with him. He wasn't getting it, so I finally just said "good night" and walked away, leaving him stunned. I'm pretty sure other women had conditioned him into thinking this was how it worked. Thankfully, I met this man when I was a little older and wiser; the younger, eager-to-please Pam would have surely gone home with him in hopes that it would morph into a long-lasting relationship.

So, how soon is too soon? I really think that depends on you and your level of emotional stability. If the physical attraction is there and you get caught up in it on the second date, it doesn't necessarily mean he will judge you or dump you. However, if he decides you're not what he's looking for and stops calling you after that, can you handle it? Can you *truly* handle it?

Not everyone can. I had one such friend that absolutely couldn't and showed her true colors after a one-night stand. It happened one night between friends. A large group of us went out together one night for a few drinks. Our group was a diverse but cohesive one. There were single women, single men, gay men, straight men, couples, etc. We knew a lot about each other, including the fact that one of the men in the group had a long-distance relationship and was struggling with where to go with it. He was still playing the field during this confusing time for him, but he had made it very clear to everyone that he was not interested in a relationship with anyone else. Although he was just a friend, many of the women in our group lusted after him, including our friend "D."

That night, at some point after our slightly buzzed group disbanded, D and the not-so-eligible bachelor disappeared. We learned the next day that they had slipped away and had had relations in the back seat of her car. Although it was their first encounter, we didn't think much of it and assumed they would be able to maintain their friendship. After all, D knew all about the other woman and knew this man had no interest in starting a relationship with anyone else.

Weeks later, we all attended a cook-out at a friend's house. Our friends who had engaged in the one-night stand were both there, friendly with each other, and everything seemed "normal"—that is, until everyone left to go home. I receive a call from D after the cook-out and the first words she uttered were "that was awkward." I was confused and asked her what it was that was awkward. She told me our friend had not acknowledged their encounter, and it angered her. I defended him, saying that his children were there, and there was no opportunity for him to "acknowledge" it. And how does someone acknowledge something like that anyway? "Hey, you, we slept together the other night, and I just want to acknowledge it."?

D went on to tell me how hurt she was at the lack of acknowledgement, so I reminded her that he was not interested in a relationship, was very open and vocal about that all along, and probably wanted to brush it under the rug. She became enraged at that point, telling me that what she had given him was a "GIFT" and that he should have had the decency to acknowledge it. A gift? I knew then that D was not someone who was emotionally wired to have a one-night stand. She had all sorts of expectations afterwards and was so disappointed and angry that she ended the friendship with him. She also felt as though the rest of us were unsympathetic to her and ended her friendships with us too.

> Take it slow, respect YOURSELF, and don't let any man push you into doing something you're not ready to do.

All this to say that most of us can't handle a one-night stand and shouldn't engage in one simply because we like a guy and are hoping it will turn into more. That's not the way to start a relationship and can ultimately hurt your chances with someone. In D's case, it even ruined a friendship. So, take it slow, respect YOURSELF, and don't let any man push you into doing something you're not ready to do.

Daddy Issues

I truly believe that daddy issues are at the root of many of our dysfunctional relationship patterns, and we must understand how deeply they have impacted us if we are to move forward. What kind of dad did you have growing up? Did you even have a dad? Did you have another father figure in your life? How were you treated? How was your mother or stepmother treated by this man? Was he involved? Did he make you feel safe? Did he make you feel loved?

Unfortunately, not everyone has had the picture perfect childhood that is sometimes depicted on TV and in children's books. Even the most well-intentioned parents can unknowingly screw up their children! All of those family dynamics you experienced growing up are what molded you into who you are today, and they can leave some very deep scars if not addressed.

I think there is a point early in everyone's childhood when we assume every family is like ours. Then as we become more aware of our surroundings and become involved with the families of friends and relatives, we realize that not all families are the same. By comparison, we then see that something's not quite right with our own. These often-flawed family dynamics are frequently the driving force behind people's behaviors. More specifically, the father-daughter relationship plays a huge part in how you conduct yourself in life and in your relationships.

There are countless daddy issues with which many of us grapple. I have a friend who appears to have it all, including a very loving, supportive family, but she suffers from low self-esteem and is as co-dependent as they come. She's beautiful, smart, kind, and close to both of her parents (who are still happily married after many years). What could have possibly gone wrong? It took me some time to unravel this particular mystery, but I finally succeeded. She shared with me that her dad, while always loving and kind, was the kind of dad who instead of congratulating her for getting a 98 on a test would harp on her relentlessly about the two points she missed. In his mind, he was being a good father and just trying to push her to do better. The reality, however, is that his words made her feel as though she was she never good enough in any aspect of her life. This struggle has led her to make some poor choices in the man department and to allow her entire self-esteem to be tied to the men in her life.

Without sharing too many details, I have some daddy issues of my own. It seems that living with an extremely critical, uninvolved, alcoholic father who is incapable of showing love will have a significant impact on a woman as well. Like everyone else, I want to be loved, but I fear it more than anyone I know. The thought of loving someone and not having them love me back the same way is terrifying to me. I prefer to be alone. It's safer that way. I've been accused of having commitment phobia, and while defensive at times, I have come to the conclusion that it's true. My self-preservation strategies have worked most of the time, but they have also forced me into seasons of complete isolation. It's a safe place to be, but it's a very lonely place to be. You have to be open to love to find it. You have to be willing to be VULNERABLE. And you have to be WHOLE.

If you're not whole right now, ask yourself why.

So, if you're not whole right now, ask yourself why. What or who created that hole in you, and how can you fill it? Although you may not have been raised by the daddy of your dreams, you (and I) need to believe there are still good men out there who will love you like you deserve to be loved. There are amazing fathers out there who will make sure your children don't have to grow up with the void that you did. But you must first contend with that void in yourself—and all of the anger and resentment that come with it. You must love yourself before you can love another.

Dating the Guy in the Spotlight

Have you ever dated or contemplated dating a guy in the spotlight? This could be an actor, a sportscaster, a musician, or in my case, a professional athlete. What an adrenaline rush. You know you're with someone that can have just about anyone he wants. He's adored by total strangers, stalked by desperate groupies, and paid handsomely for what he does. He's probably wealthy, charismatic, and quite possibly, devastatingly handsome. What more could a woman ask for? In my case, a LOT more.

I met Mr. Professional Athlete in a bar (and yes, you will see this "theme" throughout the book—don't judge). I went to his game and then headed out with friends afterwards, having no idea the team would be out that night as well. One of the girls was celebrating a work accomplishment, so we splurged and bought some champagne. After imbibing to our hearts' content, we ventured into the crowd, looking for trouble. With a bit of liquid courage, I became fearless, confident, and funny. I started a conversation with said athlete, and a brief "relationship" ensued.

I felt as though I had found the Holy Grail and couldn't wait to share my "accomplishment" with the world. I knew many women that wanted to be me. I felt the envy and adoration. I could also feel people looking at me wondering what I had that he wanted. I asked myself that same question. I didn't know the answer then, but I think I know now (hindsight 20/20).

Let me clear something up for you right now. A hook-up is NOT a date. A booty call is NOT a date. A series of booty calls does NOT a relationship make. I was being used, but I was too stupid to know it and NOT confident enough to hold out for what I deserved. In my twisted mind, I was being treated like a queen. No, he didn't ask me out on any "official dates." No, he never introduced me as his girlfriend. No, he never took me out in public. HOWEVER, he was sweet to me before, during, and sometimes after our "meetings." I felt cared for and loved. I felt special. Why? Because he was someone I had put up on a pedestal high above myself. He may have earned that spot in the hockey arena, but he NEVER earned that spot with me and didn't deserve it.

When you date someone like this, you not only get to date him, but you get to hang out with the other players. You get to see how they live. You get to hang out with the other chosen women. You are part of the "in crowd." What I hadn't considered is what I liked about him besides the fact that he was good-looking and in the spotlight. He was very sweet but not very bright.

One of my friends talked me into going to one of his away games during that time. I told her I didn't want to go because he would possibly see me and think I was just another groupie following him. It would make me look needy and desperate. (I *was* needy and desperate, but I didn't want *him* to know that.) But she talked me into it, saying he would never see me in the crowd and would never even know I was there. I believed her and agreed to go.

We arrived at the arena early since we had never been there before. (We bought our tickets having no idea what the layout was or where we would be sitting.) When we finally found our seats, we realized they were directly behind the penalty box. Seriously? This was quite possibly a seat that would not only get me noticed but put me in the spotlight. What happened next? You guessed it. The first penalty of the game went to my guy. Of course it did! I was squirming as he skated towards us. I even considered running or ducking, but it was too late. Busted! He grinned at me from the other side of the plexiglass and took his seat. Did I mention there was a slap shot later in the game that sent the puck flying into the air only to end up landing in my lap? Yup. EVERYONE saw me at the game. EVERYONE.

Later that evening, my friend and I headed back home and went to a local bar for a few drinks. We knew there was a chance the players would show up there eventually and waited patiently with the other groupies. Several members of the team finally showed up, including my guy. He saw me immediately and came racing over to me to say, "I seen ya at the game." I seen ya? I SEEN ya? My friend, an accomplished attorney and scholar, never let me forget it and would call me up after that just to say "I seen ya." I knew then that I had dropped my standards for superficial reasons. My type was usually someone educated and well spoken, someone with a good handle on grammar. Someone that would never say "ain't," use a double negative, or say "I seen ya." But I had overlooked all of it because of who he was and, of course, what he looked like.

So, while it can be very exciting to date someone who is famous in their own right, whether he's a professional athlete, actor, anchorman, or reality TV star, it is not a recipe for success unless you're certain that this man is still for you even if stripped of all his impressive titles. Be honest with yourself and your motivations. Don't pursue a relationship with someone just to elevate your own status. Try not to get caught up in superficial nonsense; instead, pursue a relationship with someone only if he possesses all of the qualities that are important to you. A relationship needs *depth* for it to last. If you're with someone just because they're "hot," you will likely be very disappointed years down the road when his looks and/or career have faded and you're stuck with Mr. I Seen Ya.

> **Don't pursue a relationship with someone just to elevate your own status.**

The Player

Like the guy in the spotlight, this guy is most likely devastatingly handsome and just has that "it" factor when it comes to luring women. He does it as more of a sport than anything and knows how to have you wrapped around his finger in no time. The player will convince you that you're the most beautiful, amazing, desired woman in the world while sleeping with your best friend. He is cunning, stealthy, and driven. His ultimate goal is to woo you into submission. He is feeding his own fragile ego at the expense of YOURS. That little voice in your head says, "Danger, abort, abort!," but he is an Adonis, and you are weak to his advances.

SNAP OUT OF IT! I know how easy it is to get sucked in against your better judgment. I have fallen victim to a player in the past. I still remember the first time I saw him. I was out at a bar with a friend, and he walked by us as we stood waiting for our drinks. We locked eyes as he walked past, and he grinned at me as though he already knew I was being sucked into the vortex. I think there may have been drool running down my chin at the time. I looked at my friend and said, "That's the best- looking man I have ever seen!" He was six-foot-three with dark hair, dark eyes, chiseled GQ features, and a beautiful pearly-white smile. We never spoke that night, but I couldn't stop thinking about him grinning at me. I obsessed about it all night, even looking at my reflection in the restroom mirror, wondering what he saw in me.

About a month later, I was out with friends at another local hotspot and turned to see the best-looking man ever looking over at me. It was

> The player will convince you that you're the most beautiful, amazing, desired woman in the world while sleeping with your best friend.

HIM! I was excited and nervous and made a mad dash to the ladies' room to reapply my lipstick. I was having a good hair night and feeling confident, so I decided to go for it. He made his way over to our group at one point and talked to me and some of the other girls in the group. Everyone was vying for his attention, so I backed off. I thought it was hopeless and didn't want to embarrass myself by acting like I had a chance.

Well, the thing about the player is that he is so used to women chasing him that he becomes intrigued by the one that doesn't. That someone was me. I don't even remember what we talked about, but I recall that the conversation flowed nicely. As the bar started emptying out, I panicked, knowing my time with Mr. GQ was limited. I came up with a brilliant solution and invited everyone, including my new crush, back to my townhome for an after-hours party. Mr. GQ was game, and I was nervously excited, wondering if I had made the right decision.

All of my friends, my dreamy hunk, and a couple of strangers who had overheard me and accepted the peripheral invite followed in their cars to my house. At the time, I was single and childless and already had a refrigerator full of beer in case a party erupted at my home such as it had this particular night. The fun continued on my patio with a sizeable group, including the two complete strangers with whom I'm still friends because of that night. The player maintained his interest in me despite other worthy opponents giving it their best shot. I was in disbelief; I still think he is the best-looking man I have ever seen, right up there aesthetically with my other top three—George Clooney, Ryan Gosling, and Channing Tatum. It took the buzz I already had from the beer to an entirely different level. I must be AWESOME!

I'm not going to get into the details of what happened next, but I recall my player whispering to me about going upstairs. The me I am today would have declined and held out for a *real* date, but the me I was then was going to take what she could get, so I agreed. This would set a precedent for the rest of our "relationship," which I would eventually realize was not okay.

Two months later, I was still seeing this man, but on his terms and mostly behind closed doors. I was out with friends one night when we ran into him around the time when I realized I deserved more. He asked about coming home with me, but I told him I was tired of "booty calls" and did not want to play anymore. The player usually calls the shots and decides when it's over, so this was devastating news to him. He spent the next hour or so convincing me that he cared about ME and loved spending time with me, with or without physical contact. I was still on the fence when he offered up proof by way of a night of just cuddling. He said he wanted to take me home and just hold me all night and talk.

My God, I believed him. I really did. Not only did this devastatingly handsome man like fooling around with me, but he liked me for ME. It's what every girl wants to hear. I was putty in his hands and agreed to go home with him. What a dumbass! It was at that moment when he spotted a friend across the bar that he wanted to talk to and went darting over there, telling me he would be right back.

I was calm, cool, and confident, giving my friends some quick tidbits about what had just gone down, when I glanced over just minutes later and noticed him making out with a girl on the other side of the bar. WTF? Seriously. WTF??? My good friend "Will" saw it at the same time and looked at me in disbelief as I started to cry. He kept saying, "Don't. Just don't. "Let's go dance and forget about him." But I couldn't. I couldn't believe someone would go to such great lengths to make me feel special only to take a sledgehammer to my heart just moments later. It shocked me, but it shouldn't have. He was not some doting, sweet, wonderful, faithful partner who cheated on me. He was just a player, and as Taylor Swift says "player's gonna play play play play play." Lesson learned. Game over.

The Married Man

Let me start by saying DON'T DO IT! Oh, and "separated" does still a married couple make, so don't do that either. I know it seems like fair game to date someone if he's going through a divorce or separation, because he or his wife already got the memo that it's over and there are no surprises; *however*, if you've ever gone through a divorce or are in the midst of one, you know it's a time of emotional turmoil. It's a time of intense reflection, pain, confusion, legal battles, and financial strains—not a time when you're thinking clearly.

We make the best choices in love when we are confident, whole, and fully available. The same goes for men. Do you want to be someone's filler girl? Someone's Ms. Right Now? Someone's Band-Aid? Then stay away from Mr. Separated.

If he's still married, you may be caught up in feeling special because this man already has someone, but he wants YOU. It's exciting, a bit naughty, and forbidden. You have to sneak around to see each other, and the sex is amazing.

So what's the problem? HE'S MARRIED! Oh yeah, that. He has to lie to people to be with you. His wife might be an amazing person and mother to his children, but she is too tired to pleasure him as often as he would like because she's busy working and changing diapers. Would you want some vixen to swoop in and get your man during a vulnerable point in your relationship?

When I was in my twenties, young and naïve, I had one very serious boyfriend and dallied in a few other relationships before and after him. Let's just say I had a "type." One of my friends described my type as "Mr. Apple Pie," and I described hers as "The Marlborough Man"—a rough, blue-collar smoker with facial hair and tats. What's strange is that she married a clean-cut engineer and couldn't be happier. Who knew? I digress. My type was very specific at that time. My type was clean cut, well educated, tall, dark-haired, and my age. He came with very little baggage. He also had never been married or had kids.

At twenty-eight, I had grown tired of the young men I was dating and some of their behavior. I had a great date with one particular man and was looking forward to seeing him again when I ran into him at a local bar the following weekend. He was drunk and making out with a girl in the middle of the crowd. When he spotted me, he looked as though he had seen a ghost. That was not how I had envisioned our second meeting going, and it was not something I could get past, so that was that.

The nice thing about being single is all that quality time you get with your friends. I was a regular at local happy hours every Friday, and I was out with some girlfriends one night at one of our favorite stomping grounds when I spotted an older, strikingly handsome man at the bar. We ended up talking to him and his friend for the rest of the night.

I learned that this man was just separating from his wife and looking for a place to live. As I stared into his beautifully chiseled face and saw the tears in his eyes as he spoke about his beloved children, I became entranced, and without warning, I found myself offering up my spare bedroom to this handsome man. We exchanged numbers and said our goodbyes. It wasn't until the next day when I realized I had offered up a room in my home to a total stranger simply because he was attractive (and I may have been slightly buzzed). I'm sure it wasn't the first time a woman has made a bad decision because of a handsome face or strong drink, but it was certainly one of my most memorable mistakes. Whoopsie!

Part of me was hoping I would never hear from him again so I wouldn't have to face the stupidity of my actions and figure out how to tell him the offer was off the table. The other part of me was dying to hear from him and occasionally fantasizing about what life would be like with this exciting new roommate.

Well, my friends, he called! I could barely breathe when I heard his voice, but I managed to keep my cool. He offered to take me to dinner so we could discuss our new living arrangement, and I agreed. When he picked me up for our date, I was excited to see he was as good-looking as I had remembered, but I was still uncertain about how to handle the roommate discussion. He was charming, warm, and incredibly funny. I was weak and succumbed to his charm immediately. I think we were halfway through dinner when I blurted out that I was way too attracted to him to let him move in. He agreed, gave me the goodnight kiss of a lifetime at the door, and made another date with me.

That was the beginning of a highly dysfunctional relationship that lasted close to three years and possibly more if you count subsequent hook-ups. Let's get back to the main issue at hand: HE WAS STILL MARRIED. But like some of you may have done before, I convinced myself that it was okay because he was separated. I learned the hard way, twice, that it's not.

This man is still a friend of mine and is a good person, but he was in a bad place in his life. I helped him through some very dark moments during his divorce. I also caught him "cheating" on me with his . . . WIFE. I didn't know how to feel because they were separated, but she was not officially his ex-wife yet, so knowing that he cheated on me with her made me feel like the "other woman." They had a very disturbing love/hate relationship that made me uneasy. He "butt dialed" me several times during our relationship while he was with her, but he always managed to talk his way out of trouble. He had a built-in excuse to be with her—their children. I was too young and inexperienced to respect that responsibility like I should have, but I was also smart enough to know there was more to it.

I have known women who intentionally pursued married men, and I believe they need help. A LOT of help. But I have also known women who very innocently fell in love with a married man and were just too weak to fight their attraction. We've all heard the excuse that "you can't help who you fall in love with." This may be true, but you CAN help whether or not you act on that love. If

If he's married, have respect for the institution of marriage, for his wife, for his family, and most of all, for YOURSELF; don't go there!

he's married, have respect for the institution of marriage, for his wife, for his family, and most of all, for YOURSELF; don't go there!

The Younger Man

Are you a cougar in the making? Do you prey on young, unsuspecting males? Have your friends nicknamed you "The Pamofile" based on past behavior? Um, yes. Let me explain.

It wasn't until my late thirties that I started to see younger men as appealing. If you're in your twenties, "younger" may mean still in college or just out of college, and that's not very appealing if you've entered adulthood and have a big girl job and a nice place to live. You're past the stage of doing keg stands and tolerating boys with naughty posters on their walls, so "younger" simply isn't an option in your mind.

However, once you're in your thirties and beyond, "younger" might just be someone with fewer miles on him— someone who is out of college, working, and established. He might be playful, attractive, fun, and baggage-free. He might be everything you used to be and still want to be. He doesn't come with children or an ex-wife (or two). He doesn't come with a beer belly. And at the end of the day, he's just plain good for your ego.

So what should you consider before getting involved with a younger man? Start by considering what it is *you* want long term and what it is *he* wants long term. If you're divorced with children and in the "been there done that" mode, it's fine to have playdates with a young hottie. Why the hell not? Men have been doing it for years. Why can't we? *But,* if this younger man has hopes for a wife and family one day, and he has fallen under your cougarific spell, that's not exactly fair to him. Just like with any relationship, it's important for both parties to know the wants and needs of the other person and to be strong enough and *selfless* enough to know when to walk away.

If you're considering dating a younger man to feed your ego, just know this plan can easily backfire on you. While it may temporarily fill a void in you and increase your self-confidence, it may also create a great deal of insecurity for which you were not prepared. Although you will both age together, the reality remains: he's always going to be younger, and you're always going to be older. That's not a big deal when he's twenty-eight and you're forty, but it may be when he's thirty-eight and you're fifty.

I was out with friends one night and spotted a handsome younger man across the room. I couldn't take my eyes off of him and felt confident enough in how I looked that night to go for it. We made eye contact several times, and I pointed him out to friends to get their approval. Since everything was based on looks at that point in my life, my friends and I all agreed he was worth pursuing. I could tell he was younger than me, but I have always felt young at heart, so I dismissed the voice in my head telling me to target someone more age appropriate and went for it.

After we exchanged a few smiles and flirted from a distance, he finally approached me. He was well groomed and well dressed with a very sophisticated look. I made many erroneous assumptions about him based solely on his appearance and was excited to meet this young stud. He was probably a hugely successful businessman with an impressive vocabulary and quick wit. He was with friends who appeared to admire him and look to him as the leader of the group. He was a force to be reckoned with, and I was ready to reckon with him.

As the young stud slowly walked towards me with a big grin on his face, I grinned back, barely able to contain myself, and tried to play it cool. Once we said our hello's and exchanged names, he began talking. It wasn't long after that when he ruined the fantasy. I wanted to shush him to keep him from saying anything more, but I didn't have the heart. After all, it was my come-hither look that started all of this, right? I don't remember a lot of the conversation, but I do remember him telling me he was a logger, and I will never forget what he said: "You're real pretty for an older lady." Whah Whah Whaaaaaaaaah. Older LADY? WHAT? Even "older GIRL" would have been better.

Notice I didn't hone in on the "real pretty" part? That's because I was subconsciously insecure about being older than him and was hoping he wouldn't notice. All I heard was "older lady," and it felt like a punch to the gut. I found an excuse to run back to my friends at some point, leaving him disappointed and bewildered. I'm sure it hurt his ego to be blown off by an older lady almost as much as it hurt my ego to be called by the same. Let's call it a lose-lose.

I'm not saying not to go for it, because you truly are awesome and look amazing for your age! I'm just suggesting you proceed with caution and understand each party's motivations. A significant age difference doesn't have to be a deal breaker if you're both mature,

> **A significant age difference doesn't have to be a deal breaker if you're both mature, consenting adults.**

consenting adults, but it can be. Just realize that he probably won't know the song they played at your senior prom and will have no idea what a landline phone is. The first "I love you" may come in the form of a text, and you will be labeled the dreaded "cougar" while he is most likely part of the most highly sought after and demographically powerful consumer group called "The Millennials. "Can you deal with it? If so, put your AARP card away and go have some fun!

Geographically Undesirable

Does absence really make the heart grow fonder? Have you ever been in a long-distance relationship or considered entering into one? Some will tell you that true love can endure any distance while other, more pessimistic types, will tell you "long distance relationships never work." Well, I'm not here to convince you of one or the other; instead, I'll share with you why this particular brand of dating can be challenging for some obvious and some not-so-obvious reasons.

My first real long-distance relationship was also my most significant relationship, so I have no regrets and learned a great deal about myself during the course of my long and somewhat complicated courtship with J. It began when he was home visiting his family one weekend, and we were both out with friends. He was tall with jet-black hair and blue eyes, which was just my type at the time (since my type back in my younger days consisted only of a physical description as compared to my type now, which is more about character). We clicked instantly and ended the night with him asking for my number (and a hot kiss goodnight in the parking lot). Unfortunately, he lived over four hours away, so our official first date would have to wait until his next trip home.

After our first date, it was obvious that this was going somewhere, so we began our long-distance courtship. Although it was difficult at times not being able to see him whenever I wanted, it was incredible when we *did* see each other. I'm a planner, and planners love to have things planned out *in advance*. So, instead of trying to juggle between my friends and my new boyfriend each weekend, I could instead have a planned weekend with my boyfriend once or twice a month and spend the rest of the time with my friends. It was working out perfectly.

About six months into our relationship, my long-distance lover moved home and began preparing for law school. I had fallen in love with him by this time and was completely blindsided one night when he told me he needed to "take some time off" from our relationship to study for the LSATs. Now, I'm a pull-that-damn-Band-Aid-off-quickly kind of girl and was *certain* this was his way of pulling it off slowly, so I asked him to leave and told him we were done (only because I thought that's what *he* was trying to do). Turns out he never did want to remove the Band-Aid. He just really wanted a few months off, but I still don't believe you can "take time off" from a relationship. You're either in it, or you're not!

I'll never forget the pain and heartbreak I felt after that break-up. It was truly excruciating and left me not wanting to make myself vulnerable ever again. Shortly after that, a man I had gotten to know from my office building asked me out. He was someone I already knew and with whom I felt safe. He was attractive, wonderful, and so good to me, but my heart still belonged to J. To make a long story short (something I clearly suck at), I made a mess out of all of it when J. came back around asking for another chance. I do have regrets about how I handled all of that, but I ultimately ended up back with my true love.

J. and I grew closer than ever after that, but he was soon off to law school, putting a long distance between us once again. Law school kept him extremely busy, as expected, so I did most of the commuting in his direction. I was back to having planned weekends again and loved it. Not only did we have to plan in advance, but we never took our time together for granted. I arrived to a candlelight dinner every Friday night. It was incredible. He was a true romantic and treated me like a princess. I appreciated it all so much, which only drove him to do more for me. Everything was wonderful, despite all the work that came along with law school (for both of us since I typed most of his papers), and his first year seemed to pass by quickly. After that, he came home for the summer and we were able to see each other more often. I was excited for him to return home and thought it would be wonderful, but I soon noticed the romance stopped. He seemed to be finding excuses to do things without me. I felt taken for granted and longed to be apart from him again so we could miss each other more.

I longed to be apart from him again? What's wrong with that statement? Everything! I should have known then and there that I had a problem. Unfortunately, it took several more long-distance relationships through the years before I realized I had an affinity for geographically undesirable men, for all the wrong reasons. J and I made it through his second year of law school and part of his third, but we broke up just before the last semester of his third year. It was somewhat mutual but initiated by me, and I was running away for all the wrong reasons.

First of all, it's human nature to take people we see every day for granted. It's not okay, but it's normal and is something couples need to work through. You see, while long-distance relationships can be great, they are not reality, and they're simply not sustainable. I became so addicted to missing someone, and having him miss me, that I overlooked amazing men in my own backyard. I didn't even realize I was doing it until a good (honest) friend accused me of having commitment phobia. HUH? I think at that point, I was "dating" someone from Belgium and couldn't believe she could say such a thing to me.

> **While long-distance relationships can be great, they are not reality, and they're simply not sustainable.**

My excuse, when my friend accused me of being afflicted with commitment phobia, was that I travel a lot and just happen to meet men from other places. The reality of the situation was that I was afraid to date locally and much more apt to give someone a chance if there was a geographic barrier between us. Whether it was my commitment issues, my need to plan ahead, or my addiction to having someone miss me, it was not leading me to a long-lasting, functional, normal relationship.

So before you entertain that long-distance relationship, consider the reasons why you're doing so and whether or not it's truly sustainable.

Dating as a Single Mom

Adding to your inbox of insecurities about yourself are now insecurities about your children—how they will react to someone new and how someone new will react to them. You'll have questions about who would want to date a single mom. Will they be okay with my limited availability? How can I possibly squeeze dating into my already hectic schedule? You or your prospective date may also have a difficult ex in the picture, further complicating the situation.

Let me start by saying this—your children come first. Let me repeat that: YOUR CHILDREN COME FIRST! I have seen lonely single moms drop their children at the first sign of love with no regard for the impact it will have on their children's immediate and long-term future. And while everyone in the equation deserves to be happy, you still need to put the needs of your children before your own and consider the impact of ALL of your actions on them. You're the adult and are much better equipped to handle change and uncertainty than they are, even if you've convinced yourself otherwise.

Once again, YOUR CHILDREN COME FIRST! I may say it one more time before this chapter is over because it's something I feel very strongly about. I have seen women so desperate to find someone new that they leave their children at home alone to go out with friends in hopes they will meet someone. I have seen women miss important events in their children's lives to go out on dates. I have seen women turn their children over to their ex-husbands more often than is required so they can be with their new boyfriends.

I recently saw a woman *move* three states away to be near her boyfriend, leaving her children behind with their father, only to move back less than two months later because it didn't work out. Sure, she's back with her children again, but the damage is done. That move, as short lived as it was, conveyed a devastating message to her children, one they will live with forever and one that will keep them wondering when she will do it again. She fell in love, and, although she loves her children unconditionally, when confronted with a difficult decision, she put her boyfriend first. No, no, NO!

These are not small sacrifices necessary to find and keep a man. These are life-altering choices that impact your children negatively and permanently. You may think they're fine, but they are seeing the most important person in their life put them on a shelf temporarily so they can spend time pursuing someone else. It makes your children feel alone, insecure, rejected, and insignificant. As a parent, you are supposed to be their rock, their caretaker, and their constant. If they can't trust you, who can they trust?

When you date as a single parent, you need to think of yourself and your children as a "package deal," but without presenting the entire package to every man right out of the gate. We have all probably heard this "package deal" stuff before, but what does it mean? It means that you should be considering your children in your choices, and the man or men you date should not only understand this, but RESPECT it. They should *want* you to go to that band concert or school play instead of being with them.

> **When you date as a single parent, you need to think of yourself and your children as a "package deal,"**

You don't need to introduce every man to your children, and absolutely shouldn't, but you need to choose wisely and make sure the men you date understand and respect your priorities (your CHILDREN). If your children's father is in the picture and has them some of the time, that's a perfect opportunity to date. If they're with you full time, you have a bit of a challenge, but one that can be overcome. If possible, try not to take time away from your kids in order to date. Get a sitter to come after their bedtime, and go on dates in the evenings. Go on dates when your kids have other plans (i.e. sleepovers, etc.). It can work, but it has to be done carefully and thoughtfully.

Again, do *not* introduce every man you date to your children. Leave your children out of it until you've already established that he's worthy. It's very confusing to children to be brought into your revolving door of men, and it can be very damaging if they're spending time with and getting attached to these men only to see them leave. Yes, it's possible that you deem someone worthy, introduce him to your children, and then find that he's not who you thought he was. Break-ups are a reality, but one you don't want to put your children through over and over again unnecessarily.

If your children are old enough to ask questions about your love life, be sure to keep your responses age appropriate and brief. Too many single parents fall into the trap of becoming friends with their children and blurring the boundaries. I've seen some women even ask their young daughters what to wear on a date or how to handle a dating situation. There are far too many pressures on children these days for you to be piling any more on their plates. Kids need to be kids and left out of "adult stuff" whenever possible. This means no badmouthing their father to them either. It's not okay and will only make them resent you in the long run. Chances are, they love you both and want to be *able* to love you both without feeling guilty about it.

So choose wisely, keep your children out of it as much as possible for as long as possible, and make sure any man you're dating seriously knows, understands, and accepts you and your children being a package deal. Otherwise, show him the door!

Ticking Clocks . . .

Have you ever settled for someone just because your biological clock was ticking, and it was almost thirty-years-old o'clock? That number was absolutely terrifying for me when I was in my twenties. You know what I mean, right? Of course you do! As women, we have so much pressure on us to settle down and start having babies while we're young and fertile. It's enough to make even the most marketable and desirable of us all lower the bar and take the next man in line for his highly sought after, invaluable, baby-making sperm.

Let's just say you've waited and are now in your thirties. Holy shit, Batman! You're thinking to yourself, "I'd better get moving on finding a baby daddy . . . now!" You've probably already done the math: if I meet him this weekend and we date for a year,

> **As women, we have so much pressure on us to settle down and start having babies while we're young and fertile.**

get engaged, and get married a year later, I will be thirty-four by then. I still remember a pivotal moment in my thirties when I began losing hope. (Or should I say, when I gave up hope.) It was a very painful moment for me and a reality that many of us face or may face at some point.

I was going through the motions of my daily weekday morning routine with *The Today Show* on in the background. I was half-listening while applying my makeup in the bathroom when I overheard a segment about fertility that piqued my interest. If I recall correctly, there was a female fertility doctor on the show, and she said something along the lines of "a woman's ability to conceive PLUMMETS after the age of 35." I literally stopped applying my war paint, walked back into my bedroom, and stared at the TV incredulously, wondering if I heard her correctly. The word *plummets* echoed through my brain like one of those blunders you utter and torture yourself with endlessly by mentally repeating the words over and over. I stood there motionless, choking back the tears as the words sank in. It was something I guess I had known on some level, but I had never quite heard it put in those terms. PLUMMETS?

From that point on, I began to mourn the idea of having children. I knew I had to come to terms with it before I turned into that person who is so immersed in her own misery that she cannot be happy for others. I wanted to be happy for others and find a way to be happy with the hand I was dealt (or not dealt). I wanted to stop picturing my fantasy life with the perfect man, two perfect children, a white picket fence, and a dog. I wanted to embrace my life as a single woman with two cats and cat lady potential. And so I did.

I remember holding one of my twin brother's twin babies years later after coming to terms with this devastating blow but feeling the hurt all over again as he nuzzled his sweet baby face into my neck. It was so hard, and if you're going through that right now, I GET it. I really do. It's awful, but it's not a reason to lower the bar; no child deserves to be married to unhappy parents that don't love each other. It is, however, a reason to motivate you to get out there and actively date instead of sitting home wallowing. I admittedly became way too comfortable being single at one point and hanging out with my handsome gay friend, the one I've been referring to as "Will." Will was the perfect substitute boyfriend with most of the perks and one obvious deficit.

As if thirty weren't hard enough with all of the baby stuff and aging stuff, I had to deal with facing forty as a single, childless woman. Noooo!! While it's becoming a much more common phenomenon, it was once the kiss of death for women everywhere at that time. At least, in my head.

I was certain that my fate was sealed and had given up on many fronts, but I decided to give myself an awesome fortieth birthday present that brought me back to life. NO, I did not have a facelift or get fillers or get an escort! I went to Vegas with friends and found a professional hair and makeup artist to make me look beautiful on my big day. It was either that or sit home alone, wallowing while gorging on popcorn, watching cheesy chick flicks, and snuggling with my cats on the couch in my sweatpants all weekend. Not an option! My trip, however, was everything I had hoped it would be. I truly came back with a renewed sense of confidence and recommend this therapy to everyone!

After that milestone birthday, I decided to start actively dating again, and before long, I met the man who would later become my husband. Without getting into all of the details, I will tell you the most shocking and awesome part of all. I got married at the ripe old age of 43, conceived a child on our honeymoon, and gave birth to a healthy baby boy at the age of 44 without ever having seen a fertility specialist of any kind. It was done the "old-fashioned" way, and I thank God every day for this miracle of mine.

Now, I don't know if that will be your fate or not, but I have shared this only because I don't want you jumping into the arms of a serial killer just because you're twenty-nine years old and are convinced this is your last chance. Women are having children later in life, and it can happen to you, so don't give up or lower your standards!

Internet Dating

I don't know what the statistics are, but I am seeing more and more people have success using this particular, and oh-so-convenient, dating method. Have you done it? Are you doing it now? If not, what are you waiting for?!

Internet dating is about casting a wide net and being open to meeting total strangers in hopes of finding true love. This method is particularly helpful for people who don't get out much, don't want to date anyone at work, and don't know how to use a cucumber to draw attention to themselves at the grocery store. You can literally sit in your PJs with your pink fuzzy slippers on and a glass of wine in hand while shopping for men. Yes . . . SHOP. I use the word *shop* because, unlike organic dating, Internet dating is going to cost you. Is it worth it? Absolutely, if you're careful and learn how to use it to your advantage.

> Internet dating is about casting a wide net and being open to meeting total strangers in hopes of finding true love.

Depending on the site you're on, the prospects can be overwhelming at first. After living in your bubble where it appears there are no available men anywhere, you log into your computer and suddenly realize they're all around you and just as eager to find love as you are.

So where do you start? In keeping with the themes of my other chapters, start by knowing yourself, LOVING yourself, and knowing what you want and don't want. Then, it takes intuition to read someone's profile, look at his picture, and know if he's someone worth getting to know a little better or not.

Just like resumes, people's profiles can be a bit misleading. People can and do falsify details in their profile in an effort to look as appealing as possible. They want to make it to the interview process and might tell a few small lies to get there. Let's start with the picture. How can a picture lie? It can lie if it's from fifteen years ago, and the person is trying to pass it off as a recent photo. It can lie if it was taken just after that expensive makeover you got for your friend's wedding last year, and you can't possibly replicate the look that the professional makeup artist gave you that day. (Yes, both men *and* women are guilty of the misleading photos.) A picture can lie if it was touched up. You get the picture. Ha, ha (pun intended).

While I truly believe that looks are the least important element of the process, they are *still* important. Whether we as women want to admit it or not, we cannot force ourselves to be physically attracted to someone we're not. Yes, the level of attraction can change once you get to know someone, but the initial attraction that motivates someone to pursue or not pursue a romantic relationship is either there, or it's not. I have been duped before, and chances are, you have too. So keep this in mind when you're posting your picture. Is it recent? Is it honest? Is it YOU? As for the men you're shopping for, I would say to look for men with multiple pictures posted (if the site allows for that). That may give you a more realistic view.

Now, what or who is in the picture or pictures he posted? Is one of them of him with a hot chick? If so, keep moving. He has only posted that to prove to you that he can land a hottie and to convey the message that he wants a hottie. If he's truly secure in himself, he doesn't need to prove that to anyone and realizes it's not relevant information. Keep moving.

Is he shirtless in any of his pictures? Really?? Can you say MEATHEAD?! I don't care if he has a six-pack, eight-pack, or twelve-pack; he doesn't need to take his shirt off until the two of you have been on several dates and are back home ready to consummate your love. While he may look confident and hot, he is likely another insecure guy trying to overcompensate for some other shortcoming by showing off his great abs.

Once you've determined there's potential for physical attraction, it's time to stop and read the profile. Does it speak to you? Does it sound like a canned sales pitch, or does it sound heartfelt and original? Does he touch on things that are important to you? If you like what you read, go for it!

Whatever the site, there will come a time when you are able to exchange emails. If he has asked you out before you even get to this point, DO NOT GO! (No, do not become pen pals for two months before taking the next step either.) Remind yourself that you are dealing with a *complete stranger*, and don't divulge any information about where you work or where you live. I don't care how comfortable he makes you feel. Don't do it.

Once you've established that you have a connection via email, I would suggest taking it to the next level within the first couple of weeks. And no, not with a text, but with a good old-fashioned phone call. I've found that the decent guys will offer up their number first and offer to call you instead if you're comfortable giving out your number. This first conversation can tell you a lot about a person. I have gotten to that point and known within the first few minutes that it wasn't going anywhere. If you both feel that way, one of you just has to end the conversation politely and tell the other to have a nice life. If only you feel that way, you might need to dodge a bullet. You can either be honest (but not *too* honest), or just take the wimpy way out like I do and say you're really busy over the next few weeks and need to get back to him. If the conversation flows and you're feeling that phone chemistry, by all means, plan to meet up IN PUBLIC.

Where should you meet your blind date? First of all, don't sign up for a meal. You could be stuck for hours sitting across from someone that is nothing like the picture, profile, or voice on the phone you were expecting. I once agreed to meet a Brad Pitt look-alike for dinner after becoming pen pals three months prior. Yes, three months prior. We even spoke on the phone once, so I was convinced this was a "qualified" lead and knew what to expect. Wrong. As I stood nervously in the lobby of the restaurant waiting for my hot date to arrive, a short, and we'll say "aesthetically challenged" (far cry from Brad Pitt) man started waving at me from the bar. While I appreciated the attention, I didn't think it would be appropriate to wave back since I was there waiting for my hot date.

It took a few more waves and the stranger walking over to me before I realized the stranger *was* my date. Our table wasn't ready, so we sat at the bar and ordered drinks. I still remember the grin on the bartender's face as he watched this disaster unfold. As I studied my blind date's face for clues to see if there was any resemblance at all to the pictures he had posted, I couldn't help but be distracted by his shockingly hideous shirt. The crisp, white, button-up shirt would have been perfectly acceptable had it not had a cartoon clown-print lining. I knew this only because his sleeves were rolled up slightly, revealing the bold print. Just wait. It gets better.

After a few uncomfortable minutes at the bar, we were escorted to our table. I wondered, as I sat down across from him, how long I could sustain my poker face. He was nice to talk to but certainly not someone I could envision myself kissing at the end of the night. At some point after we ordered, he took the liberty of standing up and coming over to sit beside me. It was an impressively bold move on his part, but excruciatingly uncomfortable for me. I didn't know how to handle it, although my body language was speaking volumes, so I told him it was easier to talk to him from across the table. It seemed like a nicer thing to say than, "Get out of my personal space, you freak." He seemed a little hurt by my unwillingness to cuddle on the first date, but he respectfully obliged and moved back to his spot across from me. Crisis averted.

Finally, after what seemed like hours, the main course arrived. I was eating as fast as I could so the date could end when I noticed my date sniffing profusely. It seemed to come on quickly and was very noticeable . . . and a bit of an appetite killer. I wondered when he would excuse himself to go blow his nose when suddenly, without warning, blood started gushing down his face and all over his fugly white clown shirt. I gasped loudly, and as he clasped his hands to his face and saw the blood, he exclaimed, "Oh, my God!" and ran for the bathroom.

I sat there alone with my goat cheese chicken for what seemed like an eternity, trying hard to ignore the stares from all around me. I can't even begin to explain the emotions I was feeling, but I decided to keep my head down and try not to laugh or cry. I was absolutely mortified, but as usual, saw the humor in the situation. When he finally returned to the table after an inordinate amount of time, he apologized profusely, and I did what I could to ease his embarrassment.

Suffice it to say, I did *not* go out with this man again, nor did I *ever* agree to a first-date dinner again or allow an email exchange to continue for more than two weeks. This experience might have sent some Internet daters running for the hills, but not me. I was determined to find love, so I continued on my quest, using all of my bad-date stories as comedic material during happy hour and all of my knowledge to better screen future prospects.

So when it's time to arrange that first date, meet for coffee or meet for drinks. Nothing more, nothing less. If you meet up at night, pick a busy place with a well-lit parking lot. Don't pick your favorite local hangout where you know all of the bartenders. It can be embarrassing and way too telling if the bartender hands you a Coors Light before you even ask for it. TRUST ME on this one.

Once you're on the date, be sure to make eye contact throughout the meeting. Don't do all the talking. Make sure to ask questions about him, and *listen intently* to his answers. *Do not* check your phone on the date unless it's a babysitter call or some other legitimate emergency. Be engaged, and be engaging. Be *yourself*, and be aware of any inconsistencies in what he's saying versus what you learned about him beforehand. Trust your gut.

If all goes well, he will ask you out again. I still feel that the second and third dates should be in a neutral location to which you both must drive. Don't let someone come to your home to pick you up unless you have really gotten to know him and know where he works and lives. Even then, you should give all of that information to a friend, along with his picture, in case anything goes south. Always better to be overly cautious than to be overly trusting, especially in the world we live in now.

Now that you're armed with all of my advice, go for it! You'll expand your dating pool exponentially and might even meet someone wonderful.

Trust Your Gut
(AND Your Friends!)

Have you ever dated one of those guys that nobody liked? Whether your friends or family members shared their feelings or not, you knew they weren't in his fan club. You could tell by their expressions when you talked about him or their behavior when he was around. Even that little voice in your head told you to run a few times, but the other voice in your head yelled, "Overruled!" Wouldn't life be so much easier if the voices in our head could agree with each other?!

Despite the mountain of evidence stacking up against this guy, you continued dating him, didn't you? Maybe there was chemistry off the charts, or perhaps, you can't stand being alone. Whatever the reason, you knew—deep down in your gut—that he wasn't right for you, but you continued to date him until everything went south.

Sometimes, we just want it so badly that we talk ourselves out of mind-blowingly obvious red flags. I have done it not once, but twice, and I am still friends with one of my "mistakes," so there are no regrets and many lessons to be learned from my missteps.

Mistake number one, herein after referred to as "MNO," came along when I was young and naïve. I was at happy hour one Friday night with friends when I first met MNO. He was twelve years older than me, an age difference I had never previously entertained, but he was incredibly handsome and had a sense of humor that attracted me from the start. The biggest red flag was that he was separated.

Aside from the usual crud that accompanies dating a man with young children who is also is in the middle of a messy divorce, there were other issues. He was a bit of a womanizer with an affinity for turbulent relationships. I was still struggling with the fact that he was not yet divorced and had three children when I learned that this was his *second* divorce. My friends were on edge and not thrilled about MNO's resume, but they remained cautiously optimistic while watching and waiting in the wings to see if this guy was as amazing as I had described him.

Mr. Amazing certainly charmed my friends and acquaintances. In fact, I think Mr. Amazing, or MNO, even charmed the pants off of one of my co-workers at one point during our troubled courtship. I remember being uneasy with her reaction to him the first time they met. She looked like a kid in a candy store when she first laid eyes on him. They seemed to have an undeniable chemistry and flirted to the point of making me uncomfortable. RED FLAG! I tried to talk myself out of it but couldn't shake that feeling that something was wrong. And in true ridiculous female fashion, I decided to let it slide with him and direct my anger towards her for flirting with my guy. Quick side bar: If there's "another woman" in the picture, the problem is with YOUR MAN, not the other woman. Chances are, she's being lied to too and might even think YOU are the "other" woman.

Just when I had finally convinced myself that there was nothing going on, MNO's "best friend" pulled me aside one night and told me the two had "hooked up." I was upset and confronted MNO, but he said it wasn't true. Why, oh why, would someone's best friend make something like that up? And if it was true, why would the guy rat his friend out? It was all very confusing, so I shoved my head aside, let my heart take the lead, and believed that it never happened.

The first Valentine's Day with my handsome new man would surely be one to remember—just not for the reasons I had hoped. He travelled a lot on business, so it wasn't unusual for him to be getting in late on a Friday night. This particular Friday night was Valentine's Day, so I was hoping he would try to get home at a reasonable hour and take me out. Instead, I received a call from him, telling me he was stuck in a meeting in Boston and wouldn't be back in time to meet up with me (as it was three hours away from where I was living at the time). I was crushed but told him I understood.

Refusing to be alone on Valentine's Day, I called my girlfriends and made plans to go to happy hour. We met shortly thereafter and didn't stay out long. So, I headed back to my lonely apartment still feeling sorry for myself when, while in the fast lane, I looked to my right and saw MNO in his car with his soon-to-be ex-wife and their children. He looked at me and I looked at him, at which time I suddenly realized I was driving onto the shoulder and about to veer off the road. I turned the wheel before crashing into a guard rail and passed him, driving as fast as I could back home. I sobbed all the way home, contemplating what I would do and what I would say to him when/if he had to balls to call. I had travelled the road to Boston many times and knew it took at least three hours (and sometimes longer during rush hour) to get home. Armed with that knowledge and the fact that he had told me less than three hours earlier that he wouldn't be back until much later, I knew something was amiss.

When I finally collected myself and called MNO, I had gone from sad to angry, wondering how the hell he would get himself out of this one. He had lied to me, and there was no way around it. When I called to confront him, not only did he pretend he never saw me on the road, but he tried to cover his tracks by telling me he had gotten back "earlier than expected" and just went to the mall with his ex and the children to buy his son new sneakers with every intention of calling me when they were done. Um . . . did he think I was born *yesterday*??? NO!

So what did I do? I broke up with him on the spot (one of many times), cried to my friends, and then took him back shortly thereafter. This pattern continued to the point of exhaustion for both me and the poor souls that had to listen to me complain endlessly about him while crying on their shoulders each time. My support team eventually announced they would no longer partake in this foolishness; I was on my own. I knew what we had was incredibly dysfunctional, but I couldn't seem to break free. So how did I finally break the spell he had over me? I moved to another state! Not because of him, but for a myriad of other reasons. It was the best thing that could have happened to us and most likely the reason why we're still friends today.

Once in my new state, I decided to really "put myself out there" more with men and date people I might not have otherwise considered. Why?

Because people were telling me I made bad choices in that department and was also very guarded and too picky. It seemed everyone had an opinion, which made me begin to question myself. That's never a good place to be.

Mistake Number Two, a.k.a. "Traffic Joe," will haunt me forever. I had a friend from back home visiting me, and we were heading back to my apartment complex after having a bite to eat. We were driving back with the windows down on a two-lane road. While stopped at a red light, the guy in the car next to us looked over at me and yelled, "You're beautiful!" I smiled and said "thank you" just as the light turned green. My friend and I giggled like school girls, noticing that this guy was slowing down so that we would stop at another light at the same time. When we did, he yelled, "What's your phone number?" My friend started yelling it out as I laughed and tried to stop her. Somehow through all of it, he got my number. What an incredible ego boost this experience was for me. I was on a high from the excitement of it all.

A few miles up the road, I signaled left to go into my apartment complex and saw that Traffic Joe was behind us, turning left too. I panicked, wondering if he was following us, until he turned down a different road in the complex. As soon as we got to my place, my phone started ringing. Of course, it was him. He lived in the same complex! We laughed about it as I thought to myself, "This must be fate." We made arrangements to meet for drinks the following week. By the way, fate will fuck with you on multiple occasions, so stop putting stock in it.

The new me was feeling brave and excited about the date, but the old me second-guessed it all, wondering how weird things would get if it didn't work out and we lived in the same apartment complex. What kind of guy asks a girl out in traffic? What do I know about him? What if he's crazy? My friends thought I was the crazy one, but they were enjoying living vicariously through me and wanted a full report on "Traffic Joe" and our first date.

We met at a popular bar/restaurant one night after work. I arrived first and ordered a drink to help take off my nervous edge. I sat sipping (guzzling) my drink and wondering if he would be as cute as

I remembered. Would he be tall? I had only seen the top half of him. Well, in walked this tall cool drink of water in a suit. He recognized me immediately and came over to greet me. I was thrilled! He definitely got an A+ in the looks department. We began chatting immediately and headed down the path of getting to know each other.

Somewhere on that path, Traffic Joe told me he was adopted. Curious as to how this may have affected him, I began asking questions as he seemed to want to talk about it. I was genuinely interested and enjoying getting to know him. I asked if he knew anything about his biological parents and if he had ever met them. He looked at me with a smirk and said, "Yes." He went on to tell me that he had connected with his biological mother a few years back. They had talked on the phone initially, and she told him that she was just a teenager when she had him, which is why she gave him up for adoption. I listened intently and tried to imagine what that would feel like and how hard it must have been for him to hear.

He continued on with the story and told me she lived out of town, but she wanted to come for a visit and would get a hotel room nearby. They planned it, and she booked her flight. He was anxious, apprehensive, and excited about it. Once she arrived and called him, they made plans to meet at a local bar. They met for drinks where they had an emotional reunion and talked for hours about his life and hers. The story was riveting, and I hung on his every word. That is . . . until it took a turn. A very strange turn.

Traffic Joe told me that his mother had become very intoxicated, so she accepted his offer of a ride back to her hotel. He walked her to her room to make sure she got in safely. I enjoyed hearing what a thoughtful gentlemen he was and wondered how the story would end. It was then that he said, "And then she made a move on me." I'm sorry, WHAT!? I

Listen to your gut, your friends, and COMMON SENSE.

gasped, thinking that was as bad as the story was going to get, when he added, "Things just got out of control from there, and I spent the night."

Wait, what!? I didn't say that, but I blurted out incredulously, "With your MOTHER?" I was hoping I had missed an important detail along the way and looked to him to clear up the confusion. He just grinned and nodded in agreement. That's some serious Jerry Springer shit right there. I can't recall what happened next, besides me yelling, "Check, please!" and getting the hell out of there. Needless to say, I didn't go out with him again. Listen to your gut, your friends, and COMMON SENSE.

Controlling or Doting?

The controlling man can be hard to spot and hard to leave. He might be the most romantic guy you've ever met. He will make you feel more loved than any other man because he wants to spend ALL of his time with you. He doesn't like going out with the guys. In fact, you're not even sure if he has any friends, but you are thankful because you don't have to compete with them. He doesn't like going anywhere without you. His agenda for the weekend is not golf and football; it's *you*. His universe revolves around you, and you convince yourself that you must be AWESOME to deserve all this attention.

Okay, so you really *are* awesome (and need to believe that in your heart of hearts), but he may be controlling (and secretly wildly insecure). The more confident you are, the more easily you will be able to spot a lack of confidence in others. Conversely, the more insecure you are, the more likely you are to attract a controlling asshole. Capiche?

How do I know this? From experience, experience, experience, and observation. It took me a while to pick up on this critical nugget of wisdom. We see it happen with nice guys too. Have you ever wondered why the sweetest men end up with the bitchiest women? It's most likely because those women are controlling and set out to find someone they can control! I saw this play out with a good friend of mine years ago. He was so kind and thoughtful and wonderful and even liked me at one point, but I was more interested in jerks back then because I was young and stupid. A controlling woman found him (not by accident) and took over. Within just weeks of dating him, she had already named their first child, instructed him to stop all communications with his female friends (i.e. me), and convinced him to trade in his manly truck for a small economy car.

So what has a controlling man done to you? Notice I didn't say *"for you"* but *"to you."* What have you LET a controlling man do to you and your life? Have you had a controlling man keep you from your friends? Have you had a controlling man keep you from having male friends? Have you let a controlling man tell you how to dress or how not to dress? Have you let a controlling man abuse you physically or psychologically? If you answered "yes" to any of these questions, then we need to talk!

Years ago, I met a girl through work that I just clicked with and whom I'll call here "Dee." I didn't know a lot about Dee, but I was drawn to her sweet, bubbly personality. She was a pretty girl that always had her hair and makeup just so, and she laughed easily, making me feel like the funniest person alive when I was with her. She talked a lot about her boyfriend, and I imagined him to be some incredible, funny, handsome guy that treated her like gold. We went to happy hour together a few times, but she was usually running off to meet her boyfriend and didn't have a lot of time for friends. I didn't mind and just enjoyed the time I could spend with my new friend.

At some point during our brief friendship, I learned that Dee liked to snow ski, so I invited her to go with me one Saturday. She told me she had to check with her boyfriend first and get back to me. I didn't question it, thinking she was just being considerate of him and making sure he hadn't already planned something for them. She came to work the next day and told me it was a go.

Our big ski weekend arrived, and I told Dee that I would just pick her up on the way. I had never been to her apartment, but I knew where it was and thought that arrangement would be most convenient. As you can probably relate, I spent time doing my hair and makeup since every venue is a potential place to meet men and since I like looking good in public no matter what. My friend was the same way and was busy putting the finishing touches on her hair and makeup as I arrived. We were just about to leave when her boyfriend dropped in unexpectedly. I expected an introduction and some friendly chit chat, but no. He took one look at her and went ballistic, questioning why she had put makeup on to go skiing. I tried to add some levity to the situation by joking about how we needed to look good to make up for our inadequacies on the slopes, but it fell on deaf ears. He was irate and completely out of control. I stood there awkwardly and nervously, wondering what to do if it continued to escalate. At one point, he grabbed her arm roughly and pulled her towards him. She fought back verbally but wasn't strong enough to fight him off physically.

Much of it is a blur as I probably tried to block it from my memory, but I remember trying to pull her away from him and somehow getting to the car with her while he continued his ugly rant.

As we drove away with Dee in tears and me in a state of shock, I thought to myself "intervention time." I tried calming her down at first and allowed her to vent, but I couldn't help but notice she was making excuses for his INEXCUSABLE behavior. I was appalled. I asked her if he had gotten physical with her before, and she said, "Yes." And before I could even respond, she asked, "What do you do when your boyfriends hit you?" I'm sorry, WHAT!? Um, they don't. I didn't hesitate. I told her that I had never been hit and would not tolerate being hit. Not once, not twice, not EVER. It's not okay, and the fact that she saw this as normal boyfriend behavior was very telling and very disturbing.

> **Oftentimes, controlling men become abusive psychologically and, in more severe cases, physically.**

Oftentimes, controlling men become abusive psychologically and, in more severe cases, physically. It starts such a dangerous cycle: controlling men are usually perpetrating this cruelty on someone who already started out with low self-esteem, and when they repeatedly push their victim to the ground—figuratively and often literally—she feels even less self-worth and begins to believe she deserves it. NOBODY deserves to be on the receiving end of abuse. NOBODY. So make sure that, before you get caught in someone's web, you can say with certainty that he is doting, not controlling.

Bait and Switch

Do unto others as you would have them do unto you. We all try to put our best self forward during the dating process, but we need to be careful to put our REAL self forward. There is no sustainability without authenticity. If you've ever watched the movie *Runaway Bride*, you get what I'm talking about. The runaway bride molded herself to be whatever she thought each man wanted her to be, and she lost herself in the process (i.e. like fried eggs trying to morph into poached eggs).

Don't convince your new man that you're wildly spontaneous when in reality you are a Type A, scheduled, Nazi control freak . . . with a Franklin Covey Day-Timer planner from 1989. (Whoops, that's me.) Do not pretend to like football when you don't know what a blitz is. Do not order a white wine spritzer to sound ladylike when you would rather be downing a pint of Guinness. Okay, okay—you get the point. Like me, you may have already been duped by a guy at some point during the courting period of champagne and caviar only to find out later that he was just another inconsiderate, belching, farting, beer-drinking, football-obsessed buffoon. It might have happened to you, but don't do it to someone else.

You must be brave enough to be yourself. This comes back to our central theme of loving yourself and valuing yourself. Our fear of rejection often keeps us from letting our guard down. And while well intended, we're compromising our authenticity in the process and unknowingly sabotaging our chance for real love.

Now, while I'm a big advocate of putting your best self forward at all times and not revealing your deepest, darkest secrets on the first date, I'm also an equal advocate of keeping it real. Just because you're not going to air all of your dirty laundry on the first date does not mean you have to be someone you're not. In poker terms, it means laying down one card at a time instead of revealing your entire hand right away. That card is still yours, so you're not being dishonest. You're just choosing not to show the rest of your cards until later.

It all sounds so easy until you find someone amazing and want to hold on to him at all costs. I think many of us are people pleasers and have a tendency to morph into the women we think they want us to be instead of being ourselves. This is so hard NOT to do. I have been very guarded in the past and have, at times, come across as extremely confident when I'm not. I have blown off men that every other woman in a 100-mile radius is dying to be with, leaving them intrigued and completely befuddled. I have been pursued by those men, not because they truly cared for me, but because they liked the chase and the challenge.

That all sounds like a clever little game I've played to get what I want, but it's really just an ineffective self-defense mechanism taken from my commitment phobia collection of self-preservation tactics. If and when I do surrender to their persistent advances, I eventually end up showing my true colors, and they inevitably lose interest. So you see, my friend, it's not clever at all, and it can lead you to prolong a lot of relationships that were never meant to go anywhere *real*.

> **Finding love and being open to love means being vulnerable.**

Finding love and being open to love means being vulnerable. That's a very frightening thought for many of us, but that fear can cripple you and keep you from growing and finding true love. If you let fear and "what ifs" lead you in this life, you won't make it very far. In fact, you might not even make it out your front door. Life is about living, taking chances, trying new things, exploring the unknown, and taking a leap of faith once in a while. If you fall down, which you will every now and then, just dust yourself off and get back up.

If you really love and value yourself, you will feel comfortable being genuine. After all, don't you want someone to want you for YOU? So don't bait him under false pretenses and then switch back to the real you once he has been hooked. Bait him with your amazing, awesome, UNIQUE, special, fan-freaking-tastic self!

Meet the Family

If you're dating someone and you think it might lead to something more serious, find a way to get to know more about his family *before* you get engaged. Like most people, he probably has a skeleton or two hanging in his closet, and you need to know about it. If he's smart, he will tell you upfront about how close he is to his family, how wonderful they are, and how well they all get along. If *you* are smart, you will know that no family is perfect and that it will take a little time to uncover those demons.

Why is this so important? Aside from his DNA, his family and childhood experiences shaped him into the man he is or isn't today. There are so many traits we pick up from our parents, both good and bad, whether consciously or unconsciously, that bleed over into our relationships. It's so important to understand the family dynamic and how it has affected him and continues to affect him. It's also important because your man's family usually becomes part of your life on some level as the relationship progresses, especially if the two of you end up married. Do you want to spend every other Thanksgiving with his family?

> **It's so important to understand the family dynamic and how it has affected him.**

Today's families can be so complicated and can have a profound impact on a child's life. Is the man you're dating the product of divorce? If so, was it handled amicably, or was there a great deal of conflict with it? Keep in mind that even the most amicable of divorces can have a huge impact on a child and usually leads to them losing time with one or both parents, bouncing back and forth between two homes, being used as a pawn, and in some cases, being separated from a sibling. If his parents were divorced, did they date a lot afterwards? Did they marry other people? Does your man have stepsiblings or half siblings? Some children develop attachment issues based on significant losses during the early part of their lives.

Were his parents married? Was he adopted? Was he raised by a single parent? Does he know who both biological parents are? Does he have a good relationship with them now? How many siblings does he have? Brothers or sisters? Is he the youngest, oldest, middle or only? Who was the disciplinarian with him when he was growing up, and *how* was he disciplined? Was there any favoritism of one sibling over another? Did his family move a lot when he was growing up? Did they have pets?

Am I suggesting you grill the crap out of him on your next date to garner all of this information? NO! And be careful not to express your opinions about his family too honestly. Your family is like your hometown. You might badmouth both all day long, but GOD FORBID someone *else* utters a negative word about your family or your hometown. You will come out swinging! No . . . gather this information *slowly over time* and, if possible, spend some quality time with the family.

Were his parents wealthy, poor, or middle classed? What were their spending habits? The questions are endless, but the answers to them can provide invaluable information about your significant other.

I dated someone at one time whose mother would simply stop talking to his father when she was angry or upset about something. And although this man recognized this pattern of communication as ineffective and dysfunctional, he used it with me on several occasions.

I dated someone whose parents took frugality to an extreme level. So instead of being reasonably frugal, he went the other way, living way beyond his means without any thought of saving money.

I have, on many occasions, dated men whose families seemed very close at first glance. In my family, we have a very difficult time expressing our love. The love is implied. I'm not sure if this is due to my Scandinavian heritage, or if we're simply freaks of nature on this front, but it has made me look at other families with envy at times, thinking they were so much closer than mine. I based this assumption on the fact that they could say "I love you" easily and hugged each other often, while my family members greeted one another with a perfectly "acceptable" shoulder chuck.

What I have come to realize over time is that the words "I love you" may sound warm and loving, but they don't always come from a place of love. Sometimes, they simply come from a place of habit or obligation. Some of the most outwardly loving families are the most dysfunctional because they're not being real with each other. They're brilliant with all of the superficial obligatory fluff, but they can't communicate effectively on a deeper level. Yes, my family has its issues, but we are there for each other through thick and thin with a bond that feels stronger than most. My family, although flawed in many ways, is absolutely incredible.

So don't discount his family just because they live five states away. While they may not have a physical hold on him, they most definitely have a psychological hold on him that you need to fully assess before taking your relationship to the next level.

The One

I once bought a book called *How to Know If You're Really in Love.* Wow. The opening line should have said, "If you had to buy this book to figure it out, YOU'RE NOT IN LOVE." Duh! I was young, stupid, and obviously *not* in love. I was in love with the *idea* of him and the idea of *us*. We met in college and had an indescribable connection. There was just something about him, but I was intimidated by his good looks. Ridiculous, I know, but I felt "safer" dating a "7" than a "9" or "10." He even asked me to leave a party with him once, and I refused. We graduated without ever consummating our crush. That was the end of it. Or so I thought.

A couple years later, I was invited to the wedding of one of my college friends who lived several hours away. I had a serious boyfriend at the time and was excited to have a date to bring to the wedding. I was a bridesmaid, so I had to leave my boyfriend in the company of strangers to perform my wedding duties. As I walked down the aisle, I glanced lovingly at my boyfriend, hoping he would notice how stunningly beautiful I looked in my taffeta rose-colored sack. As I looked his way, I was totally shocked to see my college crush sitting NEXT to him. What the . . . ? I nearly tripped over my shiny bridesmaid gown. I didn't know he was invited, nor would I have guessed he would have driven five hours to get there only to end up sitting *next to my boyfriend*. Wow!

Did we hook up? What? Shame on you! I was with my boyfriend, so he was off limits. We exchanged pleasantries at the reception, and that was the end of it. All it did was stir the romantic inside of me. Cut to a few years later when I drove back to Boston to visit the same friend. Her marriage was on the rocks, unbeknownst to me, so she made plans for us to meet up with an ex-boyfriend of hers who lived in the area. Against all odds, my crush happened to be friends with him and was visiting him that very same weekend, so the four of us had a night out. Sparks flew once again, but nothing happened. We had a great night out and said our goodbyes, wondering when we would ever see each other again.

I moved out of state a few years later, never to return. My chances of seeing said crush again were slim to none. And then came our ten-year college reunion. I had just moved several states away to find work and to escape my lonely single existence in upstate New York. The same college friend whose wedding I was in called me to see if I would consider flying home for the reunion. Without hesitation, I said "No." I was single, unemployed, and living in my sister's basement. HELL NO. With any reunion, you want to show up looking amazing and bragging about your fabulous life, perfect man, and kick-ass job. She knew this would be a tough sell after I explained the reason for my resistance, so she brought out the big guns. She asked if I would go if she were to find my crush and talk him into going. Ummmm. Game changer! HELL YEAH! And so began her Internet investigation. She found several numbers (back when land lines were still popular) and finally found him. She asked him if he was going to the reunion and mentioned my name. Not only did he agree to go, but he asked for my phone number. BAM! And that's how it's done! Oh wait, let me finish . . .

The first phone call lasted several hours and led to him flying to Georgia to see me. A relationship was born. Unfortunately, the reality did not measure up to the fantasy. I felt something missing from the start, but I was convinced that we were brought together by some cosmic destiny and had the greatest story ever. It continued for quite some time until I finally realized we were not a match, and this was not fate. While I still loved the idea of how our romance unfolded, I hated the idea of being with him long term. It had to end.

I spent many years looking for "The One" with the belief that I would know immediately. He would have a glowing halo over his head. I would see fireworks when we kissed. Our chance meeting would be so fate-like and unlikely that we would just know—instinctively *know*, without having to go through the usual trials and tribulations of dating. Perhaps I watched a few too many cheesy chick flicks back in the day.

Some believe there is not just "one" person for you but many. I'm not sure what to believe anymore, but I see relationships in a much more realistic light now that I'm older. I don't want to be a buzz kill and take those romantic notions from you. I think it's great to be a hopeful romantic. It might keep you from settling, but it also might keep you from true love if you're expecting perfection.

Every relationship takes work. Yes, some make it look easier than others, and some have to work at it harder than others. I honestly believe that if you find the right partner, your "ONE," the work will be minimal but still required. Spending years with the same person can be wonderful as long as you both make a daily concerted effort not to take the other for granted and to keep the flame burning.

> **Instead of thinking about every prospect as a possible "One," take it one day at a time, and really get to know someone before slapping that label on him.**

Instead of thinking about every prospect as a possible "One," take it one day at a time, and really get to know someone before slapping that label on him. It takes time to get to know someone, and it's time well spent, regardless of the outcome, as long as you learn from every relationship. Remind yourself of how many times you thought someone could be the "One" only to find out later he was just like all the rest. Better yet, think of *yourself* as the "One," and know that Mr. Right will eventually stumble upon you if you love yourself and put yourself out there.

Exit Gracefully

If a relationship doesn't work out, don't let that diminish your self-worth or incent you to behave in an unladylike fashion. Some people just don't work together. It doesn't make either of you a bad person. It just wasn't a fit for one or both of you. If someone breaks your heart or, at the very least, bruises your ego, walk away gracefully. The best "revenge" is to move forward, learn from it, and become an even better version of yourself.

I hate even using the word *revenge* because it has such a negative connotation, and there is never a need for that, no matter how badly you were wronged. Don't ever stoop to someone else's level. You're wounded and not thinking straight. Take time to grieve and lean on friends. Take the time to think about signs you might have missed along the way. Take time to get your mojo back and improve your fabuliciousness! Learn from it. Grow from it. HEAL from it.

One of my friends used to handle rejection by saying to the man, "It's your loss." She was always so proud of herself for saying it and would let everyone know that she managed to get those parting words in via text, phone call, or email after the break-up. It was harmless (for the most part) but unnecessary and not entirely true. I don't care how awesome you are; it's not always a loss for the other person. You just might not have been his type of awesome. It may actually be a win for him to be without you. Maybe he was a couch potato and your endless energy exhausted him. Maybe your awesomeness was too much for him and made him feel bad about himself, so he had to cut you loose. Maybe he slept with your best friend because he's insecure and just needed to know he could. Just move on!

Several years back, I met a girl at work and became an acquaintance of hers after several fun and interesting conversations about "boys." I've always been a sucker for "girl talk" and believe in giving everyone the benefit of the doubt when you first meet them. Unbeknownst to me, this girl was the vengeful-stalker type. You can't always spot this type in the crowd and most certainly don't ever want to be this type. NO! She seemed like a lovely, well-adjusted, confident woman. So how did I know she was the vengeful-stalker type? I didn't . . . at first. One day, as we were chatting at the office, she told me about a man she had recently started dating and how excited she was about him. I listened intently and expressed my excitement for her. But when I followed up with her just a few short weeks later, things had changed.

This new acquaintance of mine came by my desk to tell me that she believed her new man was cheating on her. I asked her if they were exclusive, and she looked at me as though I had two heads. She went on to tell me that she does not share men with other women and wasn't having it. I explained to her that in the early stages of dating, there may be some "overlap." I think it's perfectly acceptable to date multiple people in the early stages of dating as long as you're not misleading anyone. Most men I know prefer NOT to put all of their eggs in one basket, while the women I know spend an inordinate amount of time finding the perfect egg so they can stop looking as soon as they do. Then, they do everything they can to keep it in the basket. Whatever your method, it's important to remember that the other party may be a multiple-egg kind of dater.

Clearly, my new friend was not a fan of dating someone who was spending time with other eggs. The next time I spoke with her, she told me she had done some "research" and found out who her new man was seeing on the side. Her research methods were totally unethical, but she had successfully unearthed the truth. She was visibly angry as she ran through the details of her investigation with me. I tried calming her down and was in total shock and disbelief as this seemingly mature and lovely woman actually contemplated keying someone's car and shared that juicy little nugget with me. WHAT? Hell, no! I wanted no part of this and tried desperately to talk her out of it. While she might get some satisfaction from damaging his beloved car and causing him pain in the process, she would ultimately be showing him that she was just another batshit crazy woman, making *all* women look bad in the process.

I thought I had talked her out of it and was feeling good about our conversation until I ran into her about a week later. I passed her in the hallway at work on my way to a meeting. Although I was with several of my colleagues, she still looked at me and used her hand to mimic a car being keyed to demonstrate that she had gone through with her threat. Or did she? I never followed up because I decided it was too risky being friends with someone that was capable of that type of behavior. GAME OVER!

There are also those women that like to put it all out there on social media. As my mom always said to me when I was younger, "Never put it in writing!" That shit's permanent! (No, my mom didn't say that second part; I did.) Nobody needs to see you spew the ugly details of a love gone wrong on their Facebook feed. You don't need to tell the world what an asshole he is; chances are, they already know or will eventually find out. Call a friend and buy a pint of Ben & Jerry's or Guinness, whichever makes you happier. Vent your little heart out. In private. Not in writing and not in public.

> **Don't degrade yourself by doing something ugly to the other person.**

So please don't degrade yourself by doing something ugly to the other person, no matter how badly he hurt you or how egregious his offense was. Use this time to build yourself back up and MOVE ON!

Keeping the Mystery Alive

Once you've snagged yourself a good man, how do you keep him? Just because you've found someone that loves you for *you*—and you finally feel comfortable farting in front of him—it doesn't mean you should.

No, I don't think a relationship should be as exhausting as dating if it's truly the real thing; however, I don't think either party should become too complacent either. Complacency can be a death sentence for businesses that operate under the premise, "If it ain't broke, don't fix it." While they continue to operate business as usual, some out-of-the-box competitor will come along and put them under. Likewise, if you're in a relationship and become too complacent, some competitor might come along and put *you* out of business.

It's not about having so little faith in the opposite sex that we have to be on our toes 24/7 to keep them from straying. It's about not taking our partner for granted and continuing to do things throughout the relationship that keep it fresh and alive.

I'll start with the obvious. Some women get so comfortable in their relationship that they stop making an effort on their physical appearance. Yes, true love means he will still love you sans hair and makeup, dressed **Don't let that t-shirt and sweatpants become your weekend uniform.** in your favorite t-shirt and sweatpants. Just don't let that t-shirt and sweatpants become your weekend uniform. He needs to be reminded of your inner *and* outer beauty regularly. I know firsthand how hard this can be if you're at home with children and don't have the time or energy to make that effort. Even then, it's important to have date nights where you can dress up and be the head turner you were when you first met.

One of my sisters has been married happily for over twenty years and is one of my relationship role models. I knew from the start when she met Mr. Right that he was the "One"; I was thrilled when she announced their engagement. Several years later, while I was visiting them, I noticed their relationship had started to look very comfortable and a bit flat. Don't get me wrong. They were perfectly content, but they appeared to be on the edge of the dreaded complacency.

I decided to make it my mission to put the spark back into their relationship and shake things up a bit. I started by nixing my sister's dress selection for her husband's annual Christmas party that year. It was a lovely floral number, one that my grandmother might have worn to the grocery store back in the day. (Sorry, Sis!) It would have been perfectly fine for a church luncheon, but not quite what I had in mind for an evening cocktail party at a fabulous hotel. My sister has never been one to call attention to her natural beauty or even fully comprehend just how beautiful she is (inside and out), so I decided to tackle her hair and makeup as well to showcase her full potential.

I asked my sister not to tell her husband about our little change of plans, and she agreed. The day of the event, I brought over a little black cocktail dress of mine and did her hair and makeup. When it was all done, she looked absolutely stunning and years younger. I waited anxiously for her husband to arrive home so I could witness his reaction. I was not disappointed. He walked through the front door, took one look at her, and exclaimed, "Wow!" as his eyes popped and his jaw dropped. I can't imagine what she felt seeing his reaction, but I know how satisfied and elated I felt seeing the look on his face and never forgot it. It was a much-needed reminder to him that his wife was not just a good mother and a nice person; she was and is a fierce head-turning woman who should never be taken for granted!

If you're a little more adventurous like me, you might also institute a private at-home "get-up night." I did this with a boyfriend of mine years ago and was thrilled with the outcome. Now, while he took get-up night a little less seriously than I did and used it as an excuse to make me laugh, I used it as an excuse to look and act like a very naughty girl named "Roxy." Roxy wore different outfits each time, leaving very little to the imagination, and usually had a wig on and enough makeup to paint the White House. Not only did Roxy look different from me, but she acted differently. She was bold, confident, and overtly sexual. My boyfriend was a nice Irish Catholic school boy who would NEVER date a Roxy, but he had no problem getting a visit from her from time to time. It became such a ritual that I actually became jealous of Roxy at one point, even accusing him of liking her more. Yes, I realize that I was Roxy and how utterly ridiculous that sounds, but I was young, naïve, and ridiculously insecure.

Years later, I dated an older man who had a bit of a wild side. I knew I had to keep things interesting to hold his attention, so I did just that. I don't recall how many times we did it, but I remember the first time like it was yesterday. We decided to meet at a bar and pretend not to know each other. It was fun, it was playful, and it was sexy as hell. We both got into the role so much that it really felt like a chance encounter with a stranger.

Now I realize that some of these ideas may be out of your comfort zone, and that's fine. Just start by ditching the sweatpants and wearing something a little more appealing. Shake up the routines. But if you're feeling a bit bolder than that, see the aforementioned ideas and go for it!

To Be Continued

We've covered a lot of ground on this journey, so let's review some of the main concepts. First of all, it's imperative that you love yourself and are comfortable being alone before you seek out a serious partner. And if you're just getting out of a relationship and think you're ready to date someone new, remember to take some time to heal first before you dip your toe in the water again.

It's always best to have some downtime before venturing back out again so you can also reflect on how things went and what you learned from your last relationship. Every experience, whether good or bad, is an opportunity for learning and growth. Yes, even if he pummeled you emotionally or physically. What did you learn from it? If you learned never to put up with it again, then you benefitted from it in some way.

Once you have yourself in order and are ready to get out there, then GET OUT THERE! If you don't want to date someone at work and you're a homebody, then try Internet dating. If you're the more social type, join a singles group or go to the local hotspots with your friends. Volunteering opportunities can also be a great way to meet someone while benefitting others in the process. Venture out of your comfort zone, and put yourself in the path of some eligible bachelors. Be open-minded and stop going for a certain "type." Just know the items on your short list (the deal breakers) and forget the rest.

Finally, once you find someone worthy of pursuing a relationship with you, be sure not to drop everything and everyone for your new man. A good, *secure* man will appreciate you maintaining some level of independence and allowing him to do the same. This is hard to do if *you* are the insecure one, which is why I suggest getting a handle on that ahead of time! There has to be an I-ness, a you-ness, and of course, the ever-important we-ness. Don't ever forget the we-ness, ladies! Hee, hee, hee . . . .

The possibilities are endless for a confident, secure woman who has her shit together! That's you, right? Yes, it is! You don't have to look like Angelina Jolie to have the men lining up for you, but you do need to feel like her! Beauty truly comes from within, so harness your inner goddess and go forth and conquer!

About the Author

Pam Johansson has always had a passion for helping people and enjoys entertaining the masses with her stories about dating. Armed with a master's degree in psychology, a background in couples counseling, and years of dating experience, Pam delivers an insightful guide to dating with her quirky sense of humor and hilarious anecdotes woven throughout the book. Pam currently resides in Suwanee, Georgia, with her son, Kyle, and is a native of upstate New York.

About the Book

Everyone needs a sounding board once in a while, especially when it comes to dating and finding love. Imagine having a conversation with your best friend and being able to laugh about all of your bad dates, cry about your lost loves, and strategize about how to land the perfect man. This book will give you all of that and more! You'll learn . . .

- How to break self-defeating patterns
- The importance of loving yourself first
- What kind of man you really want
- How to get the man you want
- How to keep the man you want

You'll come away with a renewed sense of confidence and a clear direction on how to date with a purpose. *You're the Prize, Not the Contestant* is a quick, easy read filled with invaluable nuggets of wisdom for the dating challenged or weary. Whether you're a rookie or a veteran in the dating arena, you'll enjoy every second of this journey and find yourself laughing out loud as the author navigates the complex world of pursuing relationships and even shares some of her own dating disasters along the way.

It's time to stop letting men run the show and acting as though they're the only prize. YOU are the prize, young lady, and don't you forget it!